100 Year Bloom

Your Keys to Living in Permanent Revival

D0916385

Written by Drs. Mahesh & Bonnie Chavda

100 Year Bloom
Your Keys to Living in Permanent Revival

Published by
Mahesh and Bonnie Chavda
P.O. Box 411008
Charlotte, NC 28241
Phone: (704) 543-7272
Fax: (704) 541-5300
info@maheshchavda.com
www.maheshchavda.com

Printed in the United States of America
ISBN 978-0-9714986-2-4

Cover Photo by Leslyn Musch

Book production by Write Hand Publishing

Contents

Our heartfelt thanks to Heather Harris,
George Payne, and our dedicated staff.
You are truly revival people.

Introduction

Exactly one hundred years ago there was an outpouring of revival glory at Azusa Street, Los Angeles, that had a global impact, ushering in a harvest of more than 600 million souls and resulting in the birth of thousands of churches.

The story of the 100 year bloom is an indication that once again God in His mercy is releasing a new season of outpouring of revival glory. The result will be the display of the works and greater works of Christ. This display of grace and miracles will potentially touch every family on earth. Zechariah 10:1 tells us to, "Ask for the rain in the time of the latter rain." Like the psalmist, we are in need of the fresh rains of the Spirit. We echo his cry as we prepare our hearts to ask for the rains of revival: "As the hart pants for the water brook, so I pant and long for You, O God" (Psalm 42:1, AMP).

Now is the time to press into God for personal and corporate revival. Over the years we have experienced times when the fire from heaven fell. On one of those occasions our good friend and mentor, Derek Prince, called it the greatest visitation he had ever experienced in his long career.

Some years ago, we saw His glory come upon certain cities in the Congo with manifestations of His miraculous power that was so amazing, that it transformed our lives and impacted multiple thousands of others who experienced it. It left us with a thirst for His presence. Nothing else on earth can satisfy once you have encountered His manifest presence. Our prayer is that as believers cry out to God in this hour in the manner of Joel 2, the outpouring of the Spirit will sweep across every family and every city on earth, resulting in the greatest harvest of souls and extraordinary miracles.

God has done it before as experienced at Cambridge, Azusa

Street, the Welsh Revival and the Second Great Awakening. Charles Finney, the leader of the aforementioned declared: "Revival is a renewal of the first love of Christians–it is an out pouring of God, causing believers to be awakened and sinners converted–it is a new beginning of obedience to God." Duncan Campbell explained: "Revival is a community saturated with God." It was reported to me that the resurrection of a little boy in the Congo under our ministry resulted in the birthing of 100 new churches. True revival is like a spiritual tsunami, or a forest fire, spreading rapidly and definitely transforming the landscape. Both young and old are impacted. I recall the baptismal service in the Congo River where we baptized, as a result of the revival, more than 3,000 in one day, men, women and children. This move was accompanied by signs and wonders, many being delivered from oppressions of sorcery and witchcraft, many blind seeing, deaf hearing and cripples walking. In the evening a sweet spirit of peace and joy would descend on these cities with thousands returning to their homes singing songs of praise and worship. We saw that "in His presence was fullness of joy." In the presence of His glory hundreds of prostitutes gave their lives to Christ, those consumed by perversion or alcohol were transformed, people made restitutions with no urging from any human source.

On one occasion the governor of a province of 12 million people was so convicted by seeing a miracle take place in front of his eyes, he repented publicly of sins including adultery and received Christ. Witnessing these and other outpourings in various areas, from the Congo to the Caribbean, has left us with a great hunger to pray in the next great move of His revival glory. It has created in our hearts a longing to remove any blockages to personal and corporate revival. Every move of God has some differences, but this we know: There is nothing like the touch of His revival presence. This book will help you in experiencing and staying in revival.

I know we are in the season for the outpouring of His latter rain. Smith Wigglesworth, the great revivalist of the last century, prophesied before his promotion to eternal glory: "I see it! I see a revival coming to planet earth as never before. There will be untold multitudes that will be saved. No man will say, 'So many and so many,' because no man will be able to count those who will come to Jesus Christ. I see it. The dead will be raised, the arthritic healed. No disease will be able to stand before God's people, and it will spread all over the world. It will be a worldwide thrust of God's power and a thrust of God's anointing. I will not see it, but you will."

May we be willing to sow in individual and corporate prayer and in fasting to reap the harvest of revival. Let us be willing to pay whatever price to usher in this outpouring. Remember: The ultimate price was paid at Calvary by Christ.

May you experience this revival and when revived, be commissioned and trained to be part of the end time army of believers who will proclaim the Good News to every nation, tribe and tongue. "Now, Lord, behold their threatenings, and grant to Your servants that we may speak with boldness Your word, by stretching forth thine hand to heal; and that signs and wonders may be done through the name of Your holy Servant Jesus." Acts 4:29-30 "For it became Him, for whom are all things, and by whom are all things in bringing many sons unto glory." Heb 2:10

Amen. So be it. Come Holy Spirit.

Dr. Mahesh Chavda

CHAPTER ONE

REVIVAL

The One Hundred Year Bloom

It is time for **Revival**

Listen to what the **Lord** is telling us now about revival, what it is, how to get it and how to **keep it**.

"O Lord, revive Your work in the midst of years!"

A land of extremes, Death Valley is a 156 mile long wasteland that lies east of the Sierra Nevada Mountains. Situated more than 280 feet below sea level, this aptly named valley is the lowest elevation in the Western Hemisphere. Characterized by barren salt flats and vast dunes interspersed with a few brave stands of scrubby vegetation, names like *Furnace Creek, Dante's View, Hell's Gate and Dead Man's Pass* dot the valley and surrounding peaks as a testimony to those who have grappled with her harshness in the past. At the peak of summer the desert floor radiates heat like an oven while the shear depth of the valley traps the air in this natural furnace, causing already fierce temperatures to soar to deadly heights. The unmerciful heat, coupled with an average rainfall of less than 2 inches per year, make this the hottest, driest climate in North America.

Early in 2005, however, all this changed when this typically barren desert burst forth with life. An unusual winter of record rains and ideal temperatures awakened seeds that had lain dormant for a century, causing a bloom of such epic proportions that experts called it a "100 Year Bloom." Desert plants produce seeds that are encased in a thick waxy coating and can lay dormant for years. This protective shell insures that the seeds only germinate when there is enough water available to flower and drop seed for a future generation. The region experienced such an unusual outpouring of rain that this arid wasteland was transformed into a colorful wonderland carpeted in yellows and purples, daisies, poppies and even several flowering varieties long-feared extinct! People flocked from all over the world just to see this amazing sight. Rangers gave guided tours to people from across the world who came to see this 100 year bloom.[1] As we ministered recently in Oregon and shared of this event, local pastors informed us that they were in the midst of experiencing prolific rains. They stated rain had not been seen to this degree for 100 years in their region.

These are signs and cycles of the Lord – prophetic signals that He uses to tell us what time it is. Keep an eye on the natural because often these events themselves are heralding the coming seasons. God is speaking to us through the deserts of Western America. The Lord brings seasons of intense rain that reaches deep into the hearts of His people and unlocks the seeds that have been lying dormant for years, even generations. Revival comes this way. Promises of God not seen for one hundred years have been waiting for the people of God to lay hold of them and step into their destiny.

One hundred years ago, the Church experienced the greatest outpouring since Pentecost in the Azusa Street Revival. Revival and the Spirit rains that fell there shifted the climate of the whole world, as evidenced by the hundreds of millions of people around the globe who call themselves Charismatics or Pentecostals. At the same time, fresh rain began to shower natural Israel. God had begun to stir the hearts of His people to return to the land of their inheritance. As the 19th century wound to an end, a fresh stirring among the Jewish communities dispersed around the globe awakened a desire to return to ancient Israel and re-establish a nation for the Jewish people. Under the leadership of visionaries such as Theodore Herzl, the Zionist movement was founded. Following the first Zionist Congress in Basle, Switzerland in 1897, Herzl wrote in his diary, *"Were I to sum up the Basle Congress in a word...it would be this: 'At Basle, I founded the Jewish State. If I said this out loud today, I would be answered by universal laughter. If not in 5 years, certainly in 50, everyone will know it."* Little did he know that it would be in exactly fifty years that his words would come to fruition! Although Herzl was not a religious Jew, he served as a catalyst that awakened the dreams of his people and planted a seed of hope of return to this land of promise. Early settlers had much to contend with – disease, poverty and a ravaged landscape, but with a dream burning in their hearts they began work to restore the land. Seeds were beginning to bloom! Dry and barren places became green; life began to spring forth in the desert as ancient Israel received back her children after centuries of empty desolation. Natural Israel remains a prophetic sign-post of the work of God and often of the enemy's frontal attack upon the church. There is a parallel restoration occurring in this age.

The coincidence of the hundred year bloom with the advent of the centennial anniversary of the Azusa outpouring and these world-changing events is a sign to the Church concerning the visitation of God upon our generation. Revival is the manifestation of spiritual seeds sown in one season bearing fruit in the next as the rain of the Spirit comes down from heaven to water fertile soil in men's hearts. The prolific rains in Death Valley brought to life rare varieties of plants whose seed were cast in a previous season of abundant rain. Likewise, the ancient seeds sown at Azusa are quivering under the soil in anticipation of the precipitation of the Spirit.

The time for the one hundred year bloom has come! It's a new season. It's a new day. This is the time for you to bloom and for the Church around the globe to bloom with revival and exhibit the glory of Christ in us. You may say, "Well, I can't possibly be in revival. The atmosphere where I live is so dark. There is so much barrenness… " But Isaiah 60:1-3 says, "Arise shine for your light has come and the glory of the Lord has risen upon you. For behold darkness shall cover the earth and deep darkness the people, but the Lord will arise over you, and His glory shall be seen upon you. Gentiles shall come to your light and kings to the brightness of your rising." Isaiah prophesies of a great revival in this chapter. Harvest, abundance, blessing, peace and joy are all fruit he describes, even as he also speaks of deep darkness covering the earth! The prophet Habakkuk prayed, "O Lord, revive Your work in the midst of the years." Then he pleads for revival at a time when all that Israel has to show for her labors is judgment, leanness of spirit and oppression. The famous end of Habakkuk's words are denoted, "a prayer of Habakkuk the prophet set to *shiggionoth*," which is a musical notation indicating wild, enthusiastic and triumphal music! He prays, "Though the fig tree does not bloom and there be no fruit on the vine; though the labor of the olive may fail and the fields yield no fruit; though the flock be cut off from the fold and there be no herd in the stalls, yet will I rejoice in the Lord. I will joy in the God of my salvation. The Lord God is my strength!"

Bible revivalists such as Habakkuk were typically those who found themselves in the dire straits of impending judgment and invasion. Their personal lives were not necessarily filled with ease or temporal happiness. Jeremiah was instructed not to marry because of the trouble to come in his generation. He lived an isolated life with few friends and was an eyewitness of the destruction and fall of Jerusalem at the hands of the Babylonians. He warned of the trouble to come for forty years. He was betrayed by his friends and rejected. Ezekiel was a contemporary of Jeremiah's. When Ezekiel's wife, "the delight of his eyes," dies, Ezekiel is commanded not to mourn or lament for her as a sign of the soon coming destruction of the temple. He languishes in Babylon while the second siege takes place in Jerusalem, and is helpless to intervene, except to be a supernatural bridge between the will of God in heaven and the works of men on earth. Joel reached his prophetic pinnacle immediately following a great natural plague that completely devastated Israel's economy. John the Baptist arose while Israel was under the boot of pagan occupiers and corrupt religious leaders. Yet, what all these men had in common, was a connection to the supernatural river coming from the throne of God. Their message, their perspective and their power came from Him. Life and circumstances were such that the prophet's revelations were just that, revelation. They were plugged into a realm that enabled them to see clearly and proclaim the work God was doing even in the midst of the dark circumstances of their day. They were revival carriers sowing seeds for future flourishing generations. These prophets understood one of the perpetual truths of the kingdom and all creation: the principle of seed time and harvest.

Nature around us gives a physical illustration of the spiritual seed God has sown into nations, into His Church and into us as individuals. We see this parallel exemplified in Isaiah 55:10-11, "For as the rain comes and the snow from heaven, and do not return there, but water the earth, and make it bring forth and bud, that it may give seed to the sower and bread to the eater, so shall My word be that goes forth from My mouth; it shall not return to Me void, but it shall accomplish what I please, and it shall prosper in the thing for which I sent it." The seeds of revival are eternal! His Word will not return void.

Like the seed time and harvest principle, the prophets sowed the seed of God's word into their generation. They had tapped into the source of revival and they were bringing down the seed of heaven and sowing it into their circumstances with the full expectancy of seeing the Word come to fruition on the earth. This is what we see in the prayer of Habakkuk "set to *shiggionoth*." This is what we see in the great men and women of faith listed in Hebrews chapter 11. This is the pattern for all who are hungry for revival. Even in the darkest hour, the Lord promises through Isaiah that "the glory of the Lord is risen upon you."

Just as we witnessed in the "hundred year bloom," despite the most desolate circumstances, there are seeds of visitation hibernating in the soil of our generation waiting for the rains of God's refreshing. The desert waste of Death Valley burst into life and yielded a harvest of those things long thought extinct until rains soaked deep into the soil where they lay. In Hosea 2:14-15 God reveals the quintessential context in which revival visits the earth: "I will allure her and bring her into the wilderness and speak to her heart. I will give her her vineyards from there. And the valley of trouble will become a door of hope." Revival is trouble that is pregnant with hope. We are standing on this threshold now. The prophetic promises and living seed inside each of us are waiting to bloom. The Lord is pouring out His Spirit on all flesh. For every person, no matter where you come from or who you are, this is the hour of your visitation. Don't miss it!

A Door of Hope

O LORD, revive Your work in the midst of years!
In the midst of the years make it known;
In wrath remember mercy.
God came from Teman,
The Holy One from Mount Paran.
His glory covered the heavens,
His brightness was like the light;
He had rays flashing from His hand,
And there His power was hidden. – Habakkuk 3:2-4

In Revelation 4 John sees a door open in heaven and a voice speaks:

After this I looked, and behold, a door standing open in heaven! And the first voice which I had heard addressing me like [the call-

14

ing of] a war trumpet said, Come up here, and I will show you what must take place in the future. At once I came under the [Holy] Spirit's power, and behold, a throne stood in heaven, with One seated on the throne! And He Who sat there appeared like [the crystalline brightness of] jasper and [the fiery] sardius, and encircling the throne there was a halo that looked like [a rainbow of] emerald. Twenty-four other thrones surrounded the throne, and seated on these thrones were twenty-four elders (the members of the heavenly Sanhedrin), arrayed in white clothing, with crowns of gold upon their heads. Out from the throne came flashes of lightning and rumblings and peals of thunder, and in front of the throne seven blazing torches burned, which are the seven Spirits of God [the sevenfold Holy Spirit]; And in front of the throne there was also what looked like a transparent glassy sea, as if of crystal. And around the throne, in the center at each side of the throne, were four living creatures (beings) who were full of eyes in front and behind [with intelligence as to what is before and at the rear of them]. The first living creature (being) was like a lion, the second living creature like an ox, the third living creature had the face of a man, and the fourth living creature [was] like a flying eagle. And the four living creatures, individually having six wings, were full of eyes all over and within [underneath their wings]; and day and night they never stop saying, Holy, holy, holy is the Lord God Almighty (Omnipotent), Who was and Who is and Who is to come. And whenever the living creatures offer glory and honor and thanksgiving to Him Who sits on the throne, Who lives forever and ever (through the eternities of the eternities), The twenty-four elders (the members of the heavenly Sanhedrin) fall prostrate before Him Who is sitting on the throne, and they worship Him Who lives forever and ever; and they throw down their crowns before the throne, crying out, Worthy are You, our Lord and God, to receive the glory and the honor and dominion, for You created all things; by Your will they were [brought into being] and were created.[2]

John stepped through that heavenly door and was immediately before the throne in the heavenly glory of revival. Like John, Israel has a rich history of looking past the tragedy of today in full expectation of the visitation to come. The valley of trouble becomes a door of hope.

A few years ago Mahesh had to undergo emergency surgery for complications that arose from scarring from a childhood appendectomy. The anesthesiologist who had administered the epidural missed a large portion where the incision was made. When Mahesh woke up in recovery, he was in excruciating pain. He cried out to the Lord and behind him, he heard the Holy Spirit say, "Turn over." With agonizing difficulty, Mahesh managed to face towards the Lord's voice. There in front of him, he saw the Western Wall in Jerusalem. In the wall, His arms outstretched stood Jesus. The Lord began to sing an amazing rock-opera symphony. Out of the song, the river of God's presence flooded Mahesh's being, filling him with joy and taking away his pain. That joyous revival river has not waned or ceased since that day. This reminds us of the promise the Lord gives us in Psalm 46, "There is a river whose streams shall make glad the city of God, the holy place of the tabernacle of the Most High."[3] This revival promise is given in the midst of a Psalm declaring that no matter what the trouble, even if the earth be removed and destruction surrounds, there is hope and refuge in God. This is best exemplified through the three week mourning period which begins with the Fast of Tammuz and culminates on Tisha B'Av, which is considered to be the saddest day on the Jewish calendar.

Tisha B'Av is a day of great fasting and mourning, an anniversary of numerous tragic events in Jewish history: This is the day the Israelites accepted the bad report of the 12 spies and caused the Lord to decree that none of that generation would enter the land of promise and possess their inheritance; This is the day the First Temple was destroyed by Babylon and millions of Jews were exiled and thousands were slaughtered; This is the day the Second Temple was destroyed by the Romans in 70 AD and another million Jews were exiled. So great was Israel's anguish the Talmud states that Mother Rachel came out of her grave and stood by the road in Bethleham weeping according to Jeremiah's prophecy.[4] This is the day that Jerusalem was plowed under and rebuilt as a pagan city by the Romans; On this day Pope Urban II declared the First Crusade, which killed tens of thousands of Jews, King Edward I ordered the expulsion of all Jews from England; in 1492, King Ferdinand set this day as the final deadline for the expulsion of all Jews from Spanish soil; during WWII, this day marked the deportation of Jews from the Warsaw Ghetto to concentration camps... and the list goes on. The period of three weeks that culminates in that terrible day, Tisha B'Av, is known as "between the straits." And it refers to the history of the Jewish people, beginning as the Egyptians chased them when they went down out of Egypt and God made a way through the Red Sea.

Interestingly on the Jewish calendar, just one week after Tisha B'Av, they celebrate a holiday whose themes are the themes of revival. It's called Tu B'Av, "the worst is behind us!" Tu B'Av indicates "the tragic love story with a happy ending." Much like the story of Hosea and his wife, Gomer, Tu B'Av depicts God's ultimate happy marriage to His covenant people. Tu B'Av is celebrated in a dance wherein young men and women find marriage partners at last. The Mishnah states, "there were no greater holidays for Israel than Tu B'Av and Yom Kippur for on them the girls of Jerusalem would go out in borrowed white dresses and dance in the vineyards. What would they say? 'Young man, lift up your eyes and see whom you choose for yourself.'"[5] Tu'B'Av was the turning point. Destruction and deprivation of the past took on restoration and new life. Tu B'Av was the celebration of reconciliation between formerly banned Benjamin and the rest of Israel. Benjamin's heinous sin and betrayal was forgiven and cleansed, promoting national unity.[6] Tu B'Av celebrated the day the generation that left Egypt ceased to die in the wilderness. It was a day of pilgrimage to Jerusalem, recognizing Jerusalem as the spiritual center of a unified Israel. On Tu B'Av the dead of Betar, the last stronghold against Roman invasion, were finally allowed burial. Tu B'Av brought closure and fulfilled righteousness. The celebrants danced and proclaimed, "The worst is behind us!" So it is when revival blooms. As a woman who has travailed to bring forth her child and, holding the baby in her arms, forgets her pain for the joy of the newborn, revival reconciles our troubled past and puts us on the threshold of our future hope. When Rachel stood by the road, weeping for her children, the Spirit of God came behind her saying, "Rachel, dry your eyes." "Refrain yourself from weepinig and your eyes from tears; for your work shall be rewarded, says the Lord, and they shall come back from the land of the enemy. There is hope for your future, says the Lord, that your children shall come back to their own border."[7] In this context, we understand Zechariah 7:3, wherein, the prophet says, "Ask the priests who were in the house of the Lord of hosts, and the prophets, saying, 'Should I weep in the fifth month and fast as I have done for so many years?'" The answer comes in Zechariah 8:18, "Then the word of the Lord of hosts came to me, saying, 'Thus says the Lord of hosts: "The fast of the fourth month, the fast of the fifth, the fast of the seventh, and the fast of the tenth, shall be joy and gladness and cheerful feasts for the house of Judah. Therefore love truth and peace." Thus says the Lord of hosts: "Peoples shall yet come, inhabitants of many cities; the inhabitants of one city shall go to another, saying, 'Let us continue to go and pray before the Lord, and seek the Lord of hosts. I myself will go also.' Yes, many peoples and strong nations shall come to seek the Lord of hosts in Jerusalem, and to pray before the Lord.'" The fullness of Israel's example to us is that for all of God's judgments, he extends more mercies. The former days of fasting and mourning for sin and calamity are washed away as God comes to His people like the rain in visitation and refreshing. He brings the object of His affection back to Himself in solidarity and love just as Hosea sought and bought back Gomer, his estranged wife.

The readings from the law and the prophets still used during the

Jewish memorials we are speaking of are revival scriptures: "Ho, everyone who thirsts come to the waters. Why do you spend your money for that which does not profit?"[8] They read Exodus 32:11-14, remembering the turning away of God's fierce wrath as He changed His mind concerning judgment He had thought to do in light of their sin. Instead, He sends revival and restores His covenant. Revival means the worst is behind us. Revival marks the end of death in the desert. Revival causes us to catch our breath and look up, knowing redemption is at hand.

It happens that during this season "between the straits," we found ourselves, like John in the Spirit on the Lord's day, standing on the threshold of an open door. The Holy Spirit gave Bonnie a prophetic message announcing the imminent revival. She declared, "the worst is behind us!" A downpour of the Spirit immersed the congregation, leaving many of the worshipers drunk in the Spirit. Eventually able to make her way home, Bonnie drove along still surrounded by the glory. *Suddenly in the passenger seat there appeared the figure of a Man.* The atmosphere was charged with spiritual electricity, light and great joy. Her whole being was surprised by the power and joy in His voice. He turned to her with a look of exuberance and shouted happily, "What is it about revival?" Bonnie relates the story in this way:

"The energy of that Heavenly Man exploded like the splash of a sudden downpour on a hot afternoon. I didn't have an answer. 'I don't know,' I said aloud. 'What is it about revival?' I asked. He replied, 'It's messy!' I remembered the scene in the church sanctuary, laughing bodies bowled over by God, enjoying His thick presence in the careless abandon of preempted schedules, lingering well after the service was over. A moment passed like a breath, and before I had time to realize all that meant He asked again, 'What is it about revival?' Knowing that 'It's messy' was not the answer He now sought, I answered back, 'Lord, I don't know. What is it about revival?' He said, 'It's spontaneous.' I thought of the four living creatures that go wherever the Spirit sends them. They are living in revival as spontaneous tuning forks, ever picking up His essence,

His power, His revelation, His sound, His vibration and His glory! It wreaks havoc. It's also glorious. The Preacher in my car asked again, 'What is it about revival?' I could only echo back, 'What is it about revival?' 'It's costly,' came the reply. I thought of everything I know about revival, about friends who have witnessed whole movements birthed out of a single service where heaven opened and came down. I thought about their lives in the days, months, and years that followed and how much it cost them. Just as I was considering the cost, the Preacher's voice thundered, 'What is it about revival? Before I could even suggest a reply, He answered, 'It's glorious! Don't be looking at what it costs. It's so glorious that you'll forget it to the farthing.'9 A fifth time He posed the question, 'What is it about revival?' Then the Preacher said, 'It's joyous!' and I began to laugh. We were almost home. I was in revival when He asked the sixth time, 'What is it about revival?' By this time, I wasn't asking back, just waiting as His answer came, 'It's rewarding!' I could feel the favor of the King of heaven on all those who were willing to embrace this messy, spontaneous, costly, glorious, joyous, rewarding revival. I considered the pearl of great price and how the man who purchased that field knew the treasure hidden in it was more valuable than all that it could cost him. Only a fool would miss such an investment opportunity! I girded myself up and made a choice to take that tiny step, a step into His glory at the throne without ever leaving home. A seventh time the Preacher asked, 'What is it about revival?' Then, 'Lord,' said I, knowing I had already learned more in those few moments than could be taught me in a year, 'What is it about revival?' I waited, the atmosphere around me changed as if this answer were the one that I should consider over all the rest...

Scripture gives us a pattern and type of revival through the prophets' descriptions of the natural response of the earth when God visits His people. This harmonious spiritual communion between God and His supreme creation creates an atmosphere charged with heaven and brings about power to affect all other realms around. Hosea declared it when his unfaithful wife, a spiritual type of God's church, changed her mind, reformed her ways and returned to him. Her turning, as will the Church's, was initiated by God, but as the object of His affection returned, the whole of creation was caught up in the love song surrounding their fresh reunion. Hosea speaks by the Spirit of God: "'In that day I will make a covenant for them with the beasts of the field, with the birds of the air, and with the creeping things of the ground...I will betroth you to Me forever...and you shall know the Lord. It shall come to pass in that day that I will answer,' says the Lord; 'I will answer the heavens, and they shall answer the earth. The earth shall answer with grain, with new wine, and with oil...Then I will sow her for Myself and have mercy...I will say to those who were not My people, 'You are My people' and they shall say, 'You are my God!'"[10] Now perhaps we can understand why the "whole of creation groans and travails to see the manifestation of the sons of God!" We have also seen glimpses of revival through the historical accounts of moves of the Spirit in the past, where whole regions and nations were transformed by His burning fire. Yet, the perfect manifestation of revival comes not from earth but from heaven. In the revelations of John, Ezekiel and Isaiah we find descriptions of the four living creatures before the throne. Mysterious, yet as powerful as the wind and somewhat like it in nature, they wheel to and fro while lightening flashes and great joyous tumult surrounds them. Holiness effuses from every bit of their beings. Shekinah fills the atmosphere around them, and the air is thick with the incense of prayer. They are in revival.

When Ezekiel saw those creatures, revival followed. The prophet was in captivity in ancient Iraq at a time of recession, depression and oppression! In that setting, the moment Ezekiel came near the throne in prayer, he saw the glory of the Lord, and like the four living creatures, he began to respond, "Holy!" Ezekiel was in revival! What changed? Only his mind! His inner man caught a revelation of God and his outer man conformed. A key to revival is that we submit our mind to the Spirit. The natural mind cannot comprehend or receive the things of the Spirit, therefore we must make a decision to bring our natural mind under the will and influence of the Spirit until it be conformed to the mind of Christ. A practical tool to accomplish this is praying in the Spirit with one's heavenly language. Perhaps you have resisted receiving your prayer language. You are living under the power and will of your carnal mind. That mind will never submit itself; you must take a step of faith and bring your mind in subjection to the things of the Spirit of God. Once Ezekiel became aware of the eternal truth of God, glorious upon His throne, his circumstances changed. The revelation of Him who governs over all gave perspective to Ezekiel's immediate experience which transformed him. Through Ezekiel, a way was opened for that experience to come down to earth in a visitation of power. This is called ushering in the glory. Though Ezekiel's contemporaries missed the immediate visitation which caught him up, the prophet's personal encounter with the glory propelled him into fulfilling destiny. This visitation made him a powerful agent of God's will on earth, affecting a nation, a generation and generations to come.

---

[1] Brian Williams. "Life Blooms in Death Valley: Wet winter creates ideal wildflower conditions," (March 15, 2005). http://www.msnbc.msn.com/id/7200952/

[2] The Amplified Bible, Revelation 4:1-11

[3] Psalm 46:4

[4] Jeremiah 31:15

[5] Mishnah: Ta'anit 4:8

[6] Judges 21:16-24   Benjamin is ostracized from the rest of the tribes. Tu B'Av marks the reconciliation between the tribes that occurs in Judges 21, when provision is made for Benjamin to find wives for their sons so that they are not cut off from the inheritance of Israel.

[7] Jeremiah 31:16-17

[8] Isaiah 55:1

[9] In Mark 12:41-44, Jesus points out the widow's offering, which the King James translates to equate to a *farthing*.

CHAPTER TWO

Revival is Messy

The Man turned to her with a look of exuberance and shouted happily, "What is it about revival?" The energy of that Heavenly Man exploded like the splash of a sudden downpour on a hot afternoon. I didn't have an answer. "I don't know," I said aloud. "What is it about revival?" He replied,

"It's messy!"

In the summer of 1983 we were pregnant with our third child. In her eighth month, Bonnie had a dream wherein she saw the region around the Soviet Union. It was very dark, but as the dream progressed, she saw tiny lights begin to spring up like flickering candles burning brighter and brighter all across the region. She recognized that she was looking at the Soviet Union and the region that is now the Ukraine. A door of emergence for those sitting in darkness waiting for the light was opening, and a great exodus from Soviet Russia was eminent. The tiny flames seemed to represent people and people groups, both Jews and Christians, that would be visited by God as Israel had been during her captivity in Egypt. They too would rise out of the darkness and shine brightly. The dream brought an acute burden for God's people living in oppression in those regions. Time and the elements travailed for exodus. God was saying to the stronghold of the enemy, "Let My people go!"

In the natural, the persecution and oppression of Soviet dissidents was coming to the forefront of the world's attention. Earlier that year, President Reagan called the Soviet Union "the evil empire." Natan Sharansky, one of millions persecuted by the regime and an imprisoned Soviet dissident that gained release in large part to prayer and the leadership of President Reagan, recounts meeting with Reagan following his release. Sharansky said, "In that first meeting with him, he told me a joke in which the General Secretary Brezhnev and Premier Kosygin, his second-in-command, were discussing whether they should allow freedom of emigration. 'Look, America's really pressuring us,' Brezhnev said, 'maybe we should just open the gates.' 'The problem is,' he continued 'we might be the only two people who wouldn't leave.' To which Kosygin replied, 'Speak for yourself.'"[1] In neighboring Ukraine, religious persecution, imprisonment and execution burned with fierceness. Suddenly, world attention focused on the plight of two Pentecostal families who were caught in the midst of the terror of this regime. The Vashnekos and the Chmykhalovs became symbols of persecution around the world. After spending five years in the U.S. Embassy in Moscow, where they had sought refuge, these families were dramatically released and allowed to emigrate. It was beginning to rain! The words of Isaiah say, "Arise, shine; for your light has come and the glory of the Lord is risen upon you." God was preparing to visit His people. Revival was on the way.

In September of that year, Mahesh would be traveling to Israel for the Feast of Tabernacles. In the throes of the dream and burdened with its significance to the impending move of God in the Soviet Union, Bonnie envisioned a banner to send with Mahesh to Israel. The tapestry would be sixteen feet high and eight feet wide – a huge flowing ensign of red velvet with the Soviet hammer and sickle upon it. Emblazoned over a background made of the images of Jews and Christians held captive, punished and persecuted, were the words of Moses to Pharoah: "LET MY PEOPLE GO!" It made a powerful statement. Bonnie, with the days of her pregnancy ticking away and a delivery date at hand, was on a mission to finish the banner in time for it to be used in the Jerusalem March and demonstration at the Kotel, where we would be crying out for the fulfillment of God's promised return of His people out of bondage. Awaiting the advent of labor pains to bring about the delivery of our child, Bonnie realized that she would need exactly two weeks beyond her delivery date to finish the banner. Once completed, it was packaged for shipping and miraculously, El Al received the huge twelve foot container for flight to the Holy Land. Literally within hours of closing the shipping container, Bonnie was on her way to the delivery room! As we arrived at the hospital, we were directed to a makeshift seating area of the busy ward. The head nurse, seasoned, tall and wearing a starched uniform and nurses' hat, informed us in her gruff demeanor that she would attend to Bonnie in a while. Bonnie explained to her, between contractions, that she was ready to deliver. The nurse raised her eyebrows and looked Bonnie up and down. "How many babies have you had?" she asked. "Two," Bonnie replied. "I have delivered hundred of babies," the woman informed us. "I'll let you know when you're ready. Sit down there!" She pointed to the hard plastic chair. "This receptionist will help you fill out your admission forms," the nurse ordered as she marched down the hall to other business.

We waited a few minutes. The receptionist at the receiving desk adjacent to the delivery room door didn't look up. "I'm ready to have this baby," Bonnie told the woman. Shuffling paperwork, the woman just nodded and smiled. "I'm ready to have this baby," Bonnie said to a passing delivery room attendant in hospital scrubs. The attendant disappeared through the delivery room doors. Bonnie looked at me and back at the lady with the papers. "I'm ready to have this baby," she insisted. I nodded and patted her arm. "Here is a pencil," I offered. Just then, our obstetrician arrived in a rush. He took one look at Bonnie and said, "Get me a stretcher! This woman is ready to have a baby!" Before I could even get scrubs over my clothes, the doctor was rolling Bonnie into an empty side room. The same head nurse was running after the stretcher blustering that she had not had time to don the prescribed over-clothes. We all collided just inside the room, and in what can best be described as a Biblically proportioned "breakthrough of waters" akin to the Lord at Perazim, our daughter Serah made her entrance into the world. That head nurse, who was so certain that she knew everything about birthing babies, stood at the end of the stretcher, drenched and dripping in amniotic fluid, attempting to hold the newborn in front of her while the doctor attended Bonnie and we waited for the necessary staff and equipment to aid in the aftermath of the birth.

Revival is organic, living and in many ways like a baby being born. Suddenly it requires everyone's attention. Revival is messy because something new that God has created has appeared in our midst. It is messy because a new thing is exactly that – something not seen before, not done exactly this way before. Like a baby, revival has the family's genetic code, but the exact features of revival are only revealed when it is born and you embrace it and fall in love with the new life granted you. Revival draws the affection of all who are alive as well as those who are being raised from the dead! The habitation of revival is as messy as its appearing. Proverbs 14:4 states, "Where there are no oxen the stall is clean…but much increase comes by the strength of the ox." Revival seems to have no respect for religious convention and tradition. Revival doesn't wait for you to arrange a schedule and put it on a calendar. It was unusual that Serah waited exactly the two weeks Bonnie needed to finish the banner. She seemed to respect the sign that she would come in the face of global events, like the labor pains already underway in the earth. But when she came, Serah didn't care if the room was ready or if she even arrived in a delivery room! Bonnie's body was compelled to cooperate with the baby's appearing at the time of birth…not the nurse's instructions or even the doctor's arrival. And although the nurse had plenty of cleaning to do, the mess was not the focus of the event. The mess came when the baby did, but the joy and wonder of the baby made us forget all about the mess. An old song says, "Turn your eyes upon Jesus. Look full in His wonderful face, and the things of earth will grow strangely dim in the light of His glory and grace!" Revival makes Jesus evident among us. Though He is there all along, revival makes Him plain. When He is made evident, all else seems tertiary and unimportant. As a woman heavy with child, the church body that is alive will give itself entirely to bringing forth and nurturing the new birth.

Revival is messy because something that was dead, and possibly well overdue, is coming to life. Imagine what it was like to be standing at the mouth of the burial cave when Lazarus, pulling at his grave clothes and frightening the religious mourners into fits, suddenly burst out. Did he still smell dead? What were those muffled shouts he was making as he pulled his mouth free from its bandages? His sisters didn't know whether to run to or away from him. As he grappled with his confining grave clothes, did he think about whether he was sufficiently dressed beneath them? All the plans for the guests and a funeral that an entire village had turned out for were suddenly called to a halt. It was a heavenly coming out party. The dead man came out of his grave and it was chaos! In like manner, revival people tend not to take note of what people think of them like they did before revival. All attention, affection and all concern is focused upon the One appearing in their midst. Revival people love and recognize the authority and presence of God, and often have little respect for the bonds and trappings of religion. They are too busy with the glorious MESS at hand. Like the children who joyously shouted the announcement of Jesus' triumphal entry to Jerusalem, revival people cry out, "Prepare the way! Blessed is He who comes in the name of the Lord!" There are always people who will oppose revival. They're dead in religion, preferring tradition, 'convenience' and order to messy revival. When the living God suddenly steps into the picture, the new features on the face of revival invade their comfort zones and threaten their control. These people, in Jesus time, sought to kill resurrected Lazarus rather than celebrate the life given back to him!

Revival is ordered chaos. In the beginning of all things "the earth was without form and void." In Hebrew, the words for "without form" and "void" are akin to that of a cataclysmic occurrence where cosmic mass collides with cosmic mass. But, all this destruction is brought to order with a word from God's mouth: "Let there be light!" Isaiah and Jeremiah, in times similar to the days of Habakkuk, use the words *tohu wa bohu* to describe conditions of confusion, emptiness, chaos, darkness and destruction that accompanies the apostasy of the people: Israel is ravaged by heathens; the temple is burned with fire — desolation brought about by God's judgment upon wickedness. All the while, the people of the covenant, full of idolatry, are religious as all get out. They cover themselves in religious decorum instead of true beauty of holiness. Like Lazarus' grave clothes, all this decorum covered, regardless of how ordered it looked, was the seething decay of death. Only revival can bring resurrection to those things that have fallen from the grace that comes with the Spirit of life.

Revival requires us to adjust our thinking and ideologies to embrace the new life in whatever manner God wants to bring it. Ezekiel, a priest who carefully kept himself according to the law, had one of his most significant encounters with God in a graveyard. The surrounding of the dead was an anathema to such as he, but like Apostle Peter's vision on the rooftop, it took a visitation to adjust the man's view and ministry. He had been sent out of a city of priests, and like a melancholy pelican mourning on a housetop, he waited alone in exile for mercy to triumph over judgment. We think of the words of David in a similar state, "You will arise and have mercy and loving-kindness for Zion, for it is time to have pity and compassion for her; yes, the set time has come, the moment designated…When the Lord builds up Zion, He will appear in His glory…Let this be recorded for the generation yet unborn, that a people yet to be created shall praise the Lord."[2] The hand of the Lord comes to Ezekiel and sets him down in a valley filled with death. "Can these bones live?" God asks His servant. Surely, from his personal perspective, Ezekiel should have answered, "No." But, like Peter on the rooftop, Ezekiel checked himself and embraced the unusual act God was about to perform, "O Lord, You know," Ezekiel answered. Then came the miracle. Not by might. Not by power. But step by step, the same rushing Spirit present at creation began His glorious work. Imagine the look on the prophet's face, eyes bulging and mouth gaping, as he sputtered out the words given him by God and saw them come to pass before his very eyes. The valley of dry bones, shaking and rattling, shifting around came one by one into formation. Like creation, the word and Spirit in the set time brings forth life. Ezekiel had no idea what was coming. He simply participated; He attended the birth! Unlike Bonnie's nurse, however, Ezekiel stood ready.

Just like Serah's arrival, Revival is Messy! The floor was drenched. Our shoes were covered. The walls dripped. The garments of the physician and the nurse clung to them. Mahesh was soaked in fluid. "I told you I was ready to have this baby," Bonnie said. The doctor looked our beautiful baby over and observed, "Hmm. This baby is exactly two weeks overdue." Just like Bonnie had asked. Life is messy. Relationships are messy. Revival is like that. Revival doesn't wait for us to ask all the advance questions, make all the preparations we think we need, take all the vital signs or fill out papers. When God is ready to do His unusual act, He does it. What we often may not have noticed is all the signs happening just beneath the surface that are precipitating the sudden outbreak of visitation. Like a deluge from rain clouds heavy with rain, like a woman in her moment of travail, revival comes suddenly. The birth of new life in the midst of God's family becomes the priority. This is a secret to welcoming revival. Revival is mysteriously connected to the glory and personal presence of God in a way the human mind may not comprehend. God, on the other hand, holds visitation as sacred, intimate communion with man. This new life is like a child, an inheritance, being granted to a barren womb.

It's messy when a baby is born. The birth itself is messy no matter who attends it. When you bring the baby home your former ways of doing things change. Schedules are disrupted. The house is often in disarray. Your priorities change. Your daily routine is nothing like it was before. The people you see, the things you talk about, the things you are interested in, and the people you want around you are new. Friends and family come to rejoice over the new arrival. They make room in their lives, as you have, to nurture and delight in the gift from heaven. All things center on the baby. Your days are full of love and wonder. The discomfort you went through is forgotten the moment that little voice coos at you the first time. Anxiety flees when you look into those precious eyes and that tiny hand grasps your finger.

It's messy when revival finally comes. But for this child we've prayed. We forget the travail of birth. The disarray in the living room is not important once the baby's home. It's messy when God gives revival. No matter how much we plan in advance to have it all together...it's going to be messy! But when it comes we forget the travail that brings down heaven's gift. And the chaos in the sanctuary is just the sign that we are alive! Receiving messy revival into our house will bring us joy unspeakable for years to come!

The believer's KEY to living in messy revival is THANKFULNESS: The way into the Presence was through the Gate of Thanksgiving. When messy revival shows up, be thankful He has come! "When there are no oxen in the stall the trough is clean but much increase comes from the strength of the ox." Proverbs 14:4.

---

[1] Natan Sharansky, *The Case for Democracy: The Power of Freedom to Overcome Tyranny and Terror* (New York: Public Affairs, 2004), 139.

[2] Psalm 102:13,16,18 The Amplified Bible

CHAPTER THREE

Revival is Spontaneous

A moment passed like a breath, and before I had time to realize all that meant, He asked again, "What is it about revival?" Knowing that "It's messy" was not the answer He now sought, I answered back, "Lord, I don't know. What is it about revival?" He said,

"It's spontaneous."

"'Behold, I send My messenger, and he will prepare the way before Me. And the Lord, whom you seek, will suddenly come to His temple, even the Messenger of the covenant, in whom you delight. Behold, He is coming,' says the Lord of hosts. 'But who can endure the day of His coming? And who can stand when He appears?'"

— Malachi 3:1-2

A few years ago we received a message of a Christian family living in a small village in New Guinea at the time the 1998 tsunami hit the island. The atmosphere in the surrounding villages was difficult for believers. But, that persecution pressed them into God and they had developed a great capacity for communing with Him. When a warning went out that a tsunami was coming, the Lord gave these believers instructions to get in their boats and row their families out to sea as far and as fast as they could. He told them, "Row toward the wave!" The idea that one would put himself and his family directly into the path of the oncoming disaster on an impression received in prayer seems incredulous to the natural mind. But the circumstances of their lives had taught those believers to trust the word of the Lord and they obeyed. As the Christians from three villages rowed their little boats seaward, the great swell of water rose on the horizon, rolling rapidly toward them. Paddling furiously into the rising tide, their hearts pounding and bodies aching from exertion, they managed to climb the wall of water and suddenly fell behind it. As the wave made land and receded, their boats were pushed far out to sea. Once the tsunami had passed, they made the day-long journey back to shore. Arriving, the Christians found much to their consternation that their villages had been devastated by the great wave. Only those who had heard the word of the Lord and obeyed survived this sudden catastrophe. One must imagine the faith it took to receive and obey the prophetic word and ROW TOWARD THE WAVE!

That wave was considered the worst of the century with its death toll rising to over 2,000 people. On December 26, 2004, a tsunami that completely eclipsed the New Guinea wave hit Phuket Island and the surrounding region. In the horrendous aftermath where initial reports indicated more than a hundred thousand lives were lost, the nations realized that the warning systems in place were completely inadequate for such an event. The addition of even a few minutes to the warning system would have saved many lives. Shocked by the reality of this catastrophic event, people are asking how it happened and what can be done to prepare in advance for future such events.

The sounds and sights of these occurrences remind us of Biblical language about the coming of the Lord. Two thousand years ago Jesus told all who would hear and prepare that these things were going to happen. He specifically mentioned earthquakes like the one that caused this great and terrible wave. He said that these signs were the "contractions" bringing forth His appearing.[1] The signs of His coming are many. One of the most recent and significant signs remains the return of the Jews to Israel out of Russia and the gentile nations where they were dispersed. Concurrent with these contractions and other "suddenlies," are times of refreshing which we call revival, harbingers of the coming great harvest at the end of the age. There are important spiritual parallels we can draw from the example of natural events like these tsunamis and the visitations of God in a generation. Let us not be caught off-guard, but let us take note of the birth pains and make the daily preparations we will need to make in advance, whether it be for revival in our generation or the coming of the Lord on the day of Christ's return.

The prophet Malachi said the Messenger of the covenant would come to prepare the way and that after Him, the Lord would suddenly come to His temple. He repeated again the warnings and announcements of earlier sages, who had watched and waited for the salvation of the Lord to visit the earth. These last prophetic words from the era that began with Moses and ended with Malachi were surely ignored by some of his contemporaries. We can assume that some of those who heard his words must have rolled their eyes in disbelief. Since the time of Noah, men had been proclaiming the same message. The skeptics may have seemed to be in the right, considering after Malachi finished speaking there was prophetic silence for four hundred years. Yet one night four centuries later, the dark sky around a little town in Judea filled with a heavenly choir. Indeed, it seemed unexpected when it came. Terrified shepherds who witnessed this advent were directed to the place of the appearing which Malachi had foretold:

"There were sheepherders camping in the neighborhood. They had set night watches over their sheep. Suddenly, God's angel stood among them and God's glory blazed around them. They were terrified. The angel said, "Don't be afraid. I'm here to announce a great and joyful event that is meant for everybody, worldwide: A Savior has just been born in David's town, a Savior who is Messiah and Master. This is what you're to look for: a baby wrapped in a blanket and lying in a manger."[2]

There had already been a confirming sign six months earlier, the birth of John the Baptist, Jesus' cousin, who would "prepare the way of the Lord." John's father was a priest of the tribe of Aaron. His neighbors and counterparts in ministry certainly witnessed the unusual signs surrounding John's birth: the priest's sudden muteness and equally sudden disappearance with the birth of his son. His first utterance was to prophesy that his son would fulfill what Isaiah had foretold, "you will go before the face of the Lord to prepare His ways,"[3] Surely, they must have seen and heard these signs indicating that the Lord was preparing to suddenly visit His people.

Fast forward to the days of John's preaching and the revival it sparked. Some were confused and uncertain of who John was and who had sent him. They reacted with reservation and suspicion. Many of them became captive to their natural minds. Revival is like that. One wonders how the word of prophecy and the sign of the priest's sudden muteness and recovery was forgotten or misinterpreted by the keepers of the promises in the temple. Some thirty years had passed between those first events and their manifestation, yet had those who lived forgotten? Had they failed to prepare their children and disciples for the revival to come? As God brings visitation in our generation, let us not be forgetful of what He has said before. Let us not be dull or slow to participate again!

There were others besides the shepherds of Bethlehem who had been watching and waiting for the Redeemer's appearing: the priest Simeon and the ancient widow Anna. Every day, for decades of their lives, Anna and Simeon had been expectantly, vigilantly preparing in hope with fasting, prayer and spiritual service for the coming of the Salvation that had been promised. Perhaps they were witnesses to Zecharia's mysterious visitation and their hearts caught fire with anticipation of the Lord's suddenly?

"And behold, there was a man in Jerusalem whose name was

Simeon, and this man was just and devout, waiting for the Consolation of Israel, and the Holy Spirit was upon him. And it had been revealed to him by the Holy Spirit that he would not see death before he had seen the Lord's Christ. So he came by the Spirit into the temple. And when the parents brought in the Child Jesus, to do for Him according to the custom of the law, he took Him up in his arms and blessed God and said: 'Lord, now You are letting Your servant depart in peace, according to Your word; for my eyes have seen Your salvation which You have prepared before the face of all people, a light to bring revelation to the Gentiles, and the glory of Your people Israel.' And Joseph and His mother marveled at those things that were spoken of Him. Then Simeon blessed them, and said to Mary His mother, 'Behold this Child is destined for the fall and rising of many in Israel, and for a sign which will be spoken against (yes, a sword will pierce through your own soul also), that the thoughts of many hearts may be revealed.' Now there was one, Anna, a prophetess, the daughter of Phanuel, of the tribe of Asher. She was of great age, and had lived with a husband seven years from her virginity; and this woman was a widow of about eighty-four years, who did not depart from the temple, but served God with fastings and prayers night and day. And coming in that instant she gave thanks to the Lord, and spoke of Him to all those who looked for redemption in Jerusalem."[4]

Jesus is the same yesterday, today and forever. We see in this, His first appearing, the nature of God's visitation in every age. There will be those who are expecting the manifestation of their faith. There will be early contractions and declarations. There will be a faithful company of believers who patiently make daily preparations for what is to come. These are the precursors, the smaller evidences like the first early birth pangs of the promised visitation. Surely others besides Simeon and Anna heard and believed the promised word, but Simeon and Anna were rowing toward the wave! One must wonder at the response of both priests and laymen to the ministry of Zacharias, Simeon and Anna. They were the advance warning system God had put in place to prepare people for the wave of His visitation. His seemingly sudden advent strained the religious system of tradition and control that many had fastened upon their lives and message. Those who had not prepared themselves to receive the visitation were washed away when it came. Some of the very ones who had heard and seen the first contractions were the ones who resisted the actual event. In fact, beginning with the forerunner ministry of John, they made themselves enemies of God and His purposes in their day. We can expect human nature and the kingdom of darkness to perpetuate the same resistance to God's appearing in every age.

The Bible describes the earth's preparation for the coming of the Lord as a woman in labor. Those who have had this experience, or been a participant in this process know that there is much daily preparation well in advance of the actual birth. If one doesn't make the necessary preparations beforehand, much stress and difficulty are added to the joyous event when the baby suddenly comes. In addition to preparing mentally and physically for the actual labor, the woman prepares herself and home for the soon coming event. She prepares the baby's nursery, she gathers the things she will need during and immediately after the birth so that when the time of arrival suddenly comes, be it in the middle of the night or at noonday, she is ready for the child to suddenly appear!

The word "suddenly" appears in Scripture in a variety of ways, but in every occurrence it carries a similar theme: visitation, the shekinah glory cloud, miracles, death, violence, deliverance from enemies, destruction aroused from God's patient anger, the advent of angels, and natural catastrophes. In those instances, "suddenly" is defined as: speedily; unexpected motion; unawares; not apparently manifest before; instantly; straightaway; toss violently as the sea with waves; in a moment; quickly; to be liquid; flow easily; in a hurry; hastily. All these descriptions are characteristics of the four living creatures the prophets saw in the glory before the throne of

God. Their nature and their bodies, as well as their commission exemplify the spontaneity manifest in revival. Revival people will have the characteristics of those four living creatures. In the coming days, take a fresh look at their example of being and resolve to dwell in the glory of the throne and He who abides there. It is time to prepare for the "suddenly." "Therefore, prepare your minds for action; be self-controlled; set your hope fully on the grace to be given you when Jesus Christ is revealed."[5] Let us set ourselves to seek the Lord in our generation, to recognize the warning signs, to receive His messengers and to be ready when His Spirit is poured out from on high in sudden visitation. Like a woman pregnant with child, we should be practicing, preparing, packing and painting the room for occupancy! And as revival surges on the horizon, remember, "**ROW TOWARD THE WAVE!**"

The believer's KEY to living in spontaneous revival is WATCH & PRAY: Jesus said 'suddenlies' would increase at the end of the age. Watching and waiting, seeking and praying, we will be prepared when He comes. "The Lord whom you seek will suddenly come to His temple!" Malachi 3:1

---

[1] Matthew 24:6-8

[2] Luke 2:8-14

[3] Luke 1:76

[4] Luke 2:25-38

[5] 1 Peter 1:13

CHAPTER FOUR

Revival is Costly

The Preacher in the car asked again, "What is it about revival?" I could only echo back, "What is it about revival?" He replied,

"It's costly!"

"In the last days perilous times will come; men will become lovers of themselves..."[1] So wrote a spiritual father to the son he had mentored. Awaiting his own martyrdom, "poured out as a drink offering," the apostle Paul writes words of counsel and strength to the son of his heart. The letter contains the heartfelt emotion of a man who made his existence an offering on the altars of devotion to God since that day he encountered the Risen Christ. A man that had once been a murderer of the very ones he is now imprisoned for, warns Timothy of the self-centeredness that shall overtake humanity as the whole earth groans in waiting for Christ's appearing at the end of the age. Paul, whose heart has been changed, as has his name, has become a vessel of sacrificial grace and miraculous power.

Prior to Christ, Paul was by birth and religious discipline considered a "Hebrew of Hebrews," perfect according to the requirements believed to make one righteous under the Mosaic law. Yet, Saul, this sworn enemy of the cross, has a personal encounter with the Light of the World that produced the man Paul who wrote the famous words: "What things were gain to me these I have counted loss for Christ. Yet indeed I count all things loss for the excellence of the foreknowledge of Christ Jesus my Lord, for whom I have suffered the loss of all things and count them as dung that I may gain Christ."[2] Encapsulating the essence of true faith in this statement, Paul exhibits the nature of God emerging in the sacrificial life of a man. He realizes that his birth, rank and accomplishments gained by a life of religious zeal had earned him little moral redemption, for God says, "I desire mercy not sacrifice." Christ has been imprinted on Paul, the former religious zealot and murderer, and in place of that misdirected zeal –agape, selfless God-love, appears.

Entering his seventh decade, Paul has been stoned, whipped, shipwrecked, before lions, imprisoned, put on trial, persecuted, rejected, often in hunger, cold and danger. Paul says the cost is small by comparison to the price Jesus paid to redeem him from eternal death. If he could live his life again, the apostle would make only one change: to have encountered Christ and embraced the high call of the gospel earlier than he did. Now at the end, Paul is sprinting toward the altar of ultimate sacrifice. The apostle looks upon the cost of gaining Christ past, present, and future with utter contentment. Nearing the finish line of his earthly race, he assures all who look to him that no matter the timing or circumstance of his fate, it is well with his soul. His mind is on those he will leave behind and he writes for their sake. Sitting in the dank darkness of a prison dungeon, with all hope of release long past and in want of even a cloak for warmth in the approaching winter, the apostle thinks of all but himself. There is not one hint of confusion of mind, bitterness of heart, or regret for the path his life has taken. There is only joy for the privilege of true sacrifice. Costly acts of sacrifice inspired by faith toward God are a reflection of the likeness, nature and glory of the One to whom they are offered. True sacrifice poses a redemptive mystery that advances the kingdom of God in every age.

What we see in the apostle was common to the faith of many in his day. How far it seems from the approach of most who claim Christ in contemporary society. Indicating his own death, Paul says he is about "to be poured out as a drink offering." Reflecting on the many instances of having offered such a sacrifice in the temple himself, his mind went back to the temple service wherein the drink offering was the final act of the offerings on the altar. Be it for sin, thanksgiving, dedication or physical healing, first was the offering of blood wherein lay redemption, for the blood sacrifices reflected Christ slain; then came grain, reflecting life in the body lain down as heaven's bread; and finally, the drink emptied out over all, reflecting mortality sown for immortality. The drink offering was the final act that sealed the sacrifice. It was the only element of the sacrifice in which no part was reserved. Unlike the other elements, no man or priest received back a portion of the drink offering for themselves; it was that which God received in full as the cup was emptied upon the altar. In like manner, Christ emptied Himself, and so, believers are called upon in every age to lay down their lives as an acceptable sacrifice on the altar of Christ.

Paul sees beyond the moment of laying down his life and reveals that he is simply "filling up the sufferings of Christ." In his mind, his life is a reasonable price for gaining Christ. In fact, his friends had warned him against going to the place where he would ultimately die. He received their warning and rebuked them, embracing the cost of redemption. You may ask, "Do Christians live like this today?" The life of a believer, as the life of Christ, is pictured in the manifold sacrifices offered daily in the temple in Jerusalem. Sacrifice was the primary expression of worship to God in the place where the shekinah cloud of God's supernatural glory rested over the mercy seat. Sacrifice was an essential requirement of the law to purchase redemption from sin. Sacrifice is essential for living in revival. Perhaps what we have failed to comprehend, as we look at this ancient sacrificial religion, is the revelation of the sacrifice of God to bring us near to Him. Sacrifice did not begin with man as worship to God. Sacrifice began with God as love for man. "For God so loved the world that He gave His only begotten Son, that whoever believes in Him should not perish but have everlasting life."[3]

The temple in Jerusalem was the center of the earth for every covenant keeper. There, all who came to commune with God, rich or poor, were welcomed as equal partners in Israel's spiritual inheritance. The rabbis teach that no sign of lack was allowed in that place of sacrifice. According to the Talmud, "There must be no sign of poverty in the abode of wealth [temple of God]."[4] The atmosphere of wealth and beauty was breathtaking. Yet, this was but an earthly copy of a heavenly temple designed around sacrifice. The temple was so impressive and such a part of the psyche of spiritual Jews that Jesus' remarks of tearing down and rebuilding their glorious temple in a matter of three days was odious. Over the ark, between the cherubim wings, in the place where God said, "I will meet with you there," was the bema or mercy seat. It was the place of ultimate communion. The rabbi's deference and the prohibition of poverty indicates not what it costs man to worship, but the value God puts on the place He has ordained for His dwelling. In fact, it is the testimony that He was willing to pay any price, even that of His most precious treasure, the only Begotten of the Father, for the redemption of the heart of man back to Himself.

Not a single unworthy or base article was found in the temple. Nothing unclean could be accepted on the sacrificial altars of worship in the temple. At the same time, we see great lengths established to receive both poor and rich persons alike to offer their sacrifices in the temple service. Clean animals offered by the poor, though small and few, were received with equal value to extensive offerings of bullocks and rams brought by the rich. This shows the blood sacrifice that Christ would make for every man, great or small. Revival welcomes all of every status and from every and any race who thirst for the Living God because He has one thing on His mind. The temple is built as a representation of the human heart and soul. It is also the gathering place of the spiritual congregation of God's covenant family. Both are created for one thing: eternal communion with Him. Ultimately, that place is the mysterious union of God with His people – Christ with His bride. It indicates the heavenly temple 'rebuilt' as the eternal dwelling place of God and man together. In the Book of Revelation, John speaks of that temple, that city, that place of worship in its ultimate perfection. In all of the opulence of the temple — 93 vessels of gold and silver; thirteen tables, nine of marble tops for the sacrifices, the rest silver and gold; the golden altar of incense; the table for the show-bread; the great golden lampstand full of scented oil — the most prized furnishing was the ark of gold hidden beyond the veil. It represented the intimate resting place God created for no one else but Himself in the heart of every man. The ark contained the testimony of God's covenant with man: manna, the bread of heavenly provision; Aaron's rod, the miraculous sign that confirmed his authority as priest and grew from the living presence of God; and the tablets of God's law, the moral framework for a blessed society.

Jews under the law were required to "appear before God" with their sacrifice a minimum of three times a year. At these appointed times, every household was to be represented in the place of communion, the temple, in person. Each of these festivals occurred in sync with important times of harvest; therefore the trip to Jerusalem meant great preparation, forethought and sacrifice on the part of all who obeyed the command. Much had to be done in advance and in the days upon return because the festivals fell when grain and fruits were being gathered for storage. The sacrifice of the feasts affected every man at the point of his livelihood. The requirement to appear before God with a sacrifice indicates our costly response to salvation in Passover; to baptism in the Spirit at Pentecost; and to keeping the faith until He comes in atonement and the final ingathering indicated by Tabernacles.

The preparations for these three pilgrimage festivals to Jerusalem took weeks. Accommodations had to be found with relatives, friends or inns, and preparations had to be made for home and fields to plan for the extended absence. In addition, preparations and purchase price for sacrificial offerings at the temple had to be made. The price incurred for those who first experienced the fulfillment of Joel 2, promised when Jesus instructed His disciples to tarry in Jerusalem, included two months of unexpected room, board and necessities beyond what they had planned for Passover, not to mention what was left further untended at home by their extended absence. So we see it was costly to usher in the first revival of the Spirit! Of the more than 400 persons Christ appeared to in His resurrected body, only a few were ultimately on hand when the promise of the Father, the Holy Spirit, was poured out.

The essence of true faith is summed up in sacrifice. Sacrifice is the cosmic law of moral redemption for the entrance of sin into creation. God's ardent intention is not religious worship, but permanent, intimate fellowship and personal communion with mankind. This intent initiates the sacrifice, as it is the only way to enter into this fellowship with Perfection. Though costly, revival will bring us into intimate communion with God. The Man in the car recalled images from Scripture that illustrate the nature of Christ in a life laid down for the sake of the things God loves. Revival is one of those things.

For much of the contemporary church, the revival experience is summed up as a one-way street of happy receivership. Perhaps that approach is why we haven't seen revival sustained as a permanent dwelling place of God's manifest presence. Perhaps that is why so many who help usher in revival wind up burned out and disillusioned. Perhaps revival is different than just intense ecstatic meetings that last for a season. It may be the portal where the Holy Spirit meets us to transport us to the next level of maturity and power in communion with Him. But, when the Man in the car said revival is costly, He went further. "Don't look at what it costs." He said, "It's so glorious that you'll forget it to the farthing."

That is very much the way true sacrifice is. Sitting with His disciples on a particular day, Jesus made a point about the sacrifice acceptable to God: "Many who were rich put in much. Then one poor widow came and put in two mites, which make a *farthing*. So He called His disciples to Himself and said, 'Assuredly I say to you this poor widow has put in more than all those who have given to the treasury; for they put in out of their abundance, but she out of her poverty put in all she had, her whole livelihood.'"[5] In offering a farthing, the widow was literally giving up her livelihood and showing her utter dependence on and trust toward God. Owning less than she needed for bare sustenance and having none to rely on for her care, she gave what she had as an offering of worship, thereby laying aside her life in His. It would have to be God who provided food, clothing and shelter now. If He did not, then the widow would have none! She was indeed living by faith. Only true love can exhibit such confidence and hope. Hers was true sacrifice and happily given.

Revival is essentially spiritual in nature, but it has a very practical side to the cost. The temple donations together with tithes and offerings provided two essential services. One was for earth, to make provision for the care and repair of the building itself and for those who ministered there. The other was service to heaven, a spiritual service to God in acknowledgement of His care and provision. These principles remain the basis for tithes and offerings given to support the church today. We might ask ourselves if our worship is that realistic, that practical, that helpful, genuine and therefore, spiritual! Jesus saw zealots of His day dividing the meticulous measures of their tithes in order to strut self-righteously. Jesus was not denouncing sacrifice in worship. He was calling for something in addition to the cost of dropping money in the collection plate. He was demanding that the temple be continually filled with vessels that lingered, labored and lived in communion with God by sacrifice. He judged their self-sacrifice as self-promotion, but not so the widow's *farthing*. He judged her gift not by its size, but by how much it had cost her.

If we are to welcome and dwell in the revival God will send, it will be in the manner of the temple sacrifice of old. Perpetual offerings upon the altars of the heart in worship and communion with God make visitation inevitable. Though it be costly, it shall surely beautify and make ready the bride Christ died for. Revival will cost us our life – not just a joyous weekend or six weeks of glory, but a lifestyle of dwelling in the temple like Simeon or Anna. They waited until they saw with their eyes what they had prayed for, and then, holding Him in their arms, they basked in the visitation when it came. Paul was a living epistle. He knew this mystery of sacrifice because of the way he had lived in intimate communion with Christ. He found His imprint in the believers he served. Of the surpassing excellence being formed in us he wrote, "But we all, with unveiled face, beholding as in a mirror the glory of the Lord, are being transformed into the same image, from glory to glory, just as by the Spirit of the Lord."[6] The image of Christ is imprinted on those who live their lives laid down in sacrificial worship of service to the One that purchased them to become His bride. Believers in the world today are still being poured out as a drink offering. Let us labor for their sakes and for the sake of all Christ loves, to lay hold of the "mystery which has been hidden from ages and from generations, but now has been revealed to His saints…to make known what are the riches of the glory of this mystery among the Gentiles which is Christ in you, the hope of glory.!"[7]

The believer's KEY to living in costly revival is FREEDOM FROM IDOLS: Revival will force idols of the heart to the surface. Sometimes a religious façade cloaks the root problem. "Those who worship Him must worship in spirit and truth." John 4:24

---

[1] 2 Timothy 3:1-2
[2] Philippians 3:-8
[3] John 3:16
[3] Babylonian Talmud, Tractate Tamid 31b
[5] Mark 12:41-44
[6] 2 Corinthians 3:18
[7] Colossians 1:26-27

CHAPTER FIVE

Revival is Glorious

As I was considering the cost of revival the Preacher's voice thundered, 'What is it about revival?' Before I could shrug He answered me,

"It's glorious!"

Lift up your heads, O you gates!
And be lifted up, you everlasting doors!
And the King of glory shall come in.
Who is this King of glory?
The LORD strong and mighty,
The LORD mighty in battle.
Lift up your heads, O you gates!
Lift up, you everlasting doors!
And the King of glory shall come in.
Who is this King of glory?
The LORD of hosts,
He is the King of glory.

— Psalm 24:7-10

The glory in Scripture, *chavod,* was a literal manifestation with physical impact by supernatural means. In the same way God filled the tabernacle, in the way He dwelt over the mercy seat in the temple, He has ordained glory to fill His entire creation — man individually and His corporate community. Science has presented us with knowledge that there is more 'empty space' occupying creation than there are particles of substance. Every kind of matter, whether solid, liquid, or vapor, consists of empty spaces in between the atoms that make up the molecules. From the grass beneath your feet to the head on your body and the air around you, creation contains empty space! This realization causes us to consider again the truth of Scripture that says, "God, who at various times and in various ways spoke in times past to the fathers by the prophets, has in these last days spoken to us by His Son, whom He has appointed heir of all things, through whom also He made the worlds; who being the brightness of His glory and the express image of His person holds all things together by the word of His power...."[1] Christ, the glory of God, holds everything together! But what is that empty space for? Why did God build it into His creation?

Nature has proven to abhor a vacuum. Empty space will be filled with something. With more empty space than particles of substance, all creation groans and travails waiting for the manifestation of God's glory that the Bible says will ultimately fill the whole earth. That empty space is the place God has reserved for Himself in everything that was made, including you. God formed an empty place in His creation so that He might infill creation with Himself to enjoy eternal intimacy and communion with the object of His desire. What a beautiful understanding of the nearness God desires with man. God intends His creation to be filled with Himself. God wants to fill your empty space and empty places with Himself and His glory! The prophet Isaiah said, "The whole earth is full of the glory of the Lord."[2] Undoubtedly it will come to pass. The name given to the Holy Spirit is *parakletos*, the One who "comes and sits in the empty place beside." As those waiting in the upper room experienced at Pentecost, He came not only to fill their meeting place, but to fill each individual vessel that had been cleansed by the blood of the covenant. Just as He did in the beginning, God by His Spirit reclaimed the *tohu wa bohu* and set about to build a habitation for Himself within His creation. How unspeakable to realize that Christ came to offer His blood for our cleansing that we might become the temple in which God resides — more glorious than those made with human hands before

The primary attribute of kings is glory. History is full of reports and legends of the glory of kings passed down through the ages. From their wealth to prowess in war, social revolution, technological innovation, and exploits in love, kings clothe themselves with glory. The King of all kings is Jesus, and according to Scripture, His glory will cover the entire earth and fill the heavens. Though there may be much about our world today that is very inglorious, those who serve Him can experience His glory now.

The glory of God is very different from the glory of earthly kings in that it is spiritual in nature. Whereas earthly kings must rely on the arm of the flesh, the *Chavod* is the substantial weight of power in God's glory that establishes His rule wherever it is manifest. Thus the glory, in all its beauty, authority, wisdom, power and wealth establishes the dominion of the King of heaven in any realm. This glory can be received, seen, and passed to others. The physical appearance of the glory is the shekinah, the fiery outshining of God resting in the cloud between the cherubim over the ark of the covenant. There at the bema, the mercy seat, God told Israel, "I will meet you there." Ultimately it was the blood poured out before the mercy seat that would cleanse the habitation God desired for Himself and, delivering His creation from empty confusion and destruction, would sanctify them as *rehoboth*, the resting place of God. It is the same for us today. God desires to meet each one of us and then to fill His people gathered together with the glory reserved for them alone. This is what happens when revival comes to stay! The death of Moses shows that is it impossible for the law to deliver the inheritance to the heirs of God's promises. For inheritance is not something earned by works of righteousness, it is bestowed through favor. But Scripture tells us the Holy Spirit has been given as a down payment or guarantee of the inheritance God has laid up for His children. That inheritance we shall fully possess at the marriage of the Lamb and after! If we follow the footprints of God from the beginning of revelation of Himself through Scripture, we find God intent upon one thing: to find a resting place for His glory, the manifest Presence of Himself by His Spirit.

The glory of a king lies in his beauty. In the case of God, His beauty is holiness, complete unadulterable consecration to all that is good and right. The prophets and revelators describe Him as having eyes of fire and a face as radiant as the light of many suns. The psalmist describes His garments as scented with all precious incense, and the Song of Songs gives Him a form such as only a palace sculptor can craft. This is called His majesty. He is our Beloved. In Scripture, His glory is described as a bright fire that can be seen with the natural eyes: it is the glory seen by Moses in the bush and on Sinai; it is the bright outshining seen by Daniel in the glorious Man and by John in the revelation of Christ; it is the cloud and pillar that followed Israel and rested over the mercy seat in the Holy of Holies; it is the whirlwind accompanied by the four living creatures that Ezekiel saw return to Jerusalem from Babylon; and it is the radiance and beauty to prepare and clothe the eternal helper of the heavenly Bridegroom as prophesied by Haggai, "The glory of the latter house shall be greater than all the former glory."[3] The glory of God is a mystery that can be experienced by believers. The glory is the refreshing and fire that comes with revival.

The glory of a king is in his authority by which he decrees a thing and it is established. In the case of God, it is *exousia*, that authority that comes only from I AM that I AM. This authority was in His word, "Let there be light," which He sent into the *tohu wa bohu* or chaos and destruction in Genesis. His authority filled the emptiness and decreed created order, life, and beauty in its midst. The *exousia* of God contains His *dunamos* power for miracles. That authority can be passed to those under authority as in the cases

of Daniel, Esther and Jesus, during His earthly ministry. His authority establishes His kingdom purposes in impossible situations. The
prophet Jeremiah decreed God's intention over captive Israel saying, "I know the plans I have for you, says the Lord, plans to give
you a future and a hope. Plans for your good and not for trouble."[4]
In the same way Jesus told His disciples, "Don't be afraid, it is the
Father's good pleasure to give you the kingdom." We should expect
to see His glory established in our lives and in the church around us.

The glory of a king is his wisdom. There is none wiser than God.
In Proverbs, wisdom is personified as the person of Jesus, present
in the beginning of creation with God just as John depicts Him in
his prologue: "The Lord possessed me at the beginning of his
way…I was brought forth while as yet He had not made the primal
dust of the world."[5] Wisdom exceeds wealth and by it kings reign
and rulers decree justice. Solomon is history's most glorious king,
exceeding all others in wealth and wisdom. He is given as a
prophetic type of Christ coming to His church in the last day. We
see in 1 Kings 4:29-31, "God gave Solomon wisdom and exceeding
great understanding, and largeness of heart like the sand of the
seashore. [His] wisdom excelled the wisdom of all the kings of the
East and of all Egypt….and his fame was in all the surrounding
nations." Yet, the Bible makes a clear distinction between the glory
of God and the glory of man. Isaiah writes, "For my thoughts are
not your thoughts, nor are your ways My ways, says the Lord."[8] In
his first letter to Corinth Paul writes, "the base things of the world
and the things which are despised God has chosen, and the things
which are not, to bring to nothing the things that are, that no flesh
should glory in His presence. But of Him you are in Christ Jesus,
who became for us wisdom from God—and righteousness and
sanctification and redemption—that, as it is written, 'He who glo-
ries, let him glory in the LORD.'"[7] The glory of God surpasses the
glory of all other kingdoms. That is why it is foolishness for man to
judge or measure the glory of God. It is more profitable to just bow
and receive it as He comes to us in the glorious rains of the revival
He sends.

The glory of God is seen in acts of His power. In Scripture these acts are two fold: miracles of deliverance from the power of enemies and wondrous works that heal and make provision. That power for miracles was the primary indicator Jesus claimed as the proof He was the sent one of God. Those miracles were a manifestation in the natural realm of the supernatural glory of God. His miracles brought joy and relief to the humble while, at the same time, they often offended and confused those who opposed Him. He still works the same way today. The glory that surrounded Israel in the wilderness and ultimately came to rest over the ark in the tent of meeting was full of signs, wonders and mighty supernatural power. That glory was a precursor to the glory ordained to indwell the Church and every believer today! However, the miracles that brought Israel's deliverance also brought judgment on Egypt. In Exodus 14:20 when the Angel of the Lord comes between the Israelites and the Egyptians, Scripture says that, "…it was a cloud and darkness to the one, and it gave light by night to the other, so that the one did not come near the other all that night." We must never forget that the glory is a two-edged sword, much like the Word of God. When the glory is revealed, it shines brightly upon all who love His appearing. But the glory also radiates power of opposition to all who oppose the kingship of Christ. His power extends the jurisdiction of His territory and fends off His enemies.

Finally the glory of kings is in their wealth. Money wields power in earthly kingdoms, but as with all authority, wealth ultimately and originally comes from God who is Alpha and Omega. Whether Jesus put the gold in the fish's mouth or knew by revelation where such a fish was and caused, by His power, Peter to catch that particular one, He is the source of all wealth. In the days of the great kings of India from whom Mahesh's mother was descended, anyone who was granted an audience with a king would also be assured of payment of all their debts, for beside their thrones the kings had treasuries of jewels and gold. At the conclusion of an audience with such a king, in benevolence befitting royalty, he would scoop out a handful of his riches and put it into the hands of his subject as they went away. When God showed His glory to Israel in Egypt, they had been in utter poverty and bondage for four hundred years. Yet, in a single night, He brought them out with silver and gold and there was none feeble in their midst.[8] The glory of God filled a nation's emptiness to overflowing through provision in the Passover lamb. As they came out and stopped for a rest, they reviewed the treasure they had been given and found it was TOO MUCH for the work they set about to do. The God of glory is the God of too much. In the same way, Christians receive wealth and riches from the Presence of the King for payment and provision for all life's troubles and debts. God gave Abraham and his lineage, of which Christians are grafted into as sons, "the power to get wealth that he might establish the covenant."

In the days of the Judges of Israel we find Gideon in the strength of his own flesh attempting to save enough food for himself and his family from the crops otherwise ravaged by Midian's army. He is cowering in the winepress when suddenly, God shows up. He greets Gideon, "Hail mighty man of valor!" On the surface Gideon appeared more like a desperate, bitter, fearful man alone. Yet in chapter 6 verse 34, the Spirit of the Lord comes upon Gideon. In our church traditions, many of us have seen this as a mantle or spiritual garment coming down over the man. This is far from the revelation of Scripture. In this passage the words literally say, "The Spirit of the Lord clothed Himself with Gideon." In other words, God put Gideon on like a glove! Now we understand how He could say, "Go in this the strength you have and save Israel as one man."

Revival glory is the mercy of God that comes as rain to refresh His inheritance when it is weary. Isaiah 4 describes this aspect of the glory, when the Branch, Jesus, is enthroned in glory as ruler over all natural and spiritual forces. His kingdom is likened to a wedding chuppa extended as a covering of glory spreading out over God's people from the place of His throne. All who come under the covering of His realm are enabled to eat its fruit: righteousness, peace and joy. It makes us think of John's vision of the new Jerusalem coming down as a bride adorned for her husband in the midst of whom, instead of the temple, is the Lamb Himself, ruling as her King. Until that day arrives, God continually seeks to overflow by the Spirit from the midst of His people, bringing visitation and revelation of Himself to people on earth so that the kingdom of God might be extended. It has been given to the Church, Jesus' glorious wife to be, to show forth this glory among the nations. When God's purpose and God's people align, revival comes and His glory is experienced.

From the beginning of time God has been longing for a glove affair with His creation! Today the Lord of heaven is asking, "May I have this dance?" See Him there, His hand extended, the nail print still visible. Lift up your vision and gaze into His eyes. Such love! Such power! Such peace! Not a shadow of condemnation or rejection. More than able to carry you. More than enough to fill your empty places. If you accept and put your hand in His, the movement of His Being to the sound of the waltz will carry you away. In His arms your feet will be drifting above the surface of this floor of earth. Keep your eyes on His as He leads you. Allow yourself to be pulled completely close, heart to His heart, your head in the cleft of His shoulder. Moses on the mountain, Gideon at the winepress, Deborah under the palms, Shunamite woman, cripple at Bethesda, leper of Samaria, master of the wedding feast in Cana. Are you running for your life? Have your dreams of destiny fled? Are your enemies destroying your crop? Is your nation oppressed? Has your child, the promise of God, died? Are the legs that were meant to carry you curled and useless? Does destruction waste your flesh? Have you run out of wine? He has saved the best for last and desires to make you glorious.

When God revealed His glory to Moses, the former adopted son of the king of the world was presently in exile for murder. All his hopes and dreams were dashed, his identity was in confusion and his very life was at stake. You may be in just such a place in your own life and circumstance today. As Psalm 102 says, the day of your trouble is the set time of God's favor. The former heir of Pharaoh was wandering behind a flock of smelly sheep in the heat of the desert of Midian. He spied a bush that burned in the distance yet somehow was not burned up. The shepherd went near out of curiosity. As he approached the amazing sight, a Voice spoke out of the fire. "Take the shoes off your feet. The ground you are standing on is holy."[9] The glory is drawing us near His unusual Presence. Hear his voice. Take off your shoes. Give Him the bitter pool, the only water you have to drink. He plans to redeem it and turn it into wine. If you will humble yourself and draw near, you will find yourself irresistibly revived and in revival. And so "Now to Him who is able to do exceedingly abundantly above all that we ask or think, according to the power that works in us, to Him be glory in the church by Christ Jesus to all generations forever and ever. Amen!"[10] He is inviting you to that dance. It's glorious! The music and the song are already playing.

The believer's KEY to living in glorious revival is to FEAR THE LORD: The fear of the Lord revives the heart and makes us responsive to His Presence at all times. "The fear of the Lord is a fountain of life." Proverbs 14:27

[1] Hebrews 1:1-3

[2] Isaiah 6:3.

[3] Haggai 2:9

[4] Jeremiah 29:11

[5] Proverbs 8:22-26

[6] Isaiah 55:8.

[7] I Corinthians 1:28-31.

[8] Psalm 105:37.

[9] Exodus 3:5

CHAPTER SIX

Revival is Joyous

*The Preacher turned and shouted joyfully, "What is it about
revival?" The thrill of His voice exploded like the splash of a sudden downpour of cool rain on a hot summer day. 'I don't know,' I
answered aloud. "What is it about revival?"*

The Preacher said, "It's joyous" and Bonnie began to laugh.

"Ask the Lord for rain in the time of the latter rain. The Lord
will make flashing clouds. He will give them showers of rain, grass
in the field for everyone." Zechariah 10:1

As a child growing up in the middle of the New Mexican desert,
Bonnie's ranch home was surrounded by an endless, arid landscape
of sagebrush, red sandstone bluffs and wide blue sky. Every spring
hot winds blew across miles of open pasture, carrying clouds of
stinging dust that would drift over the top of the five-foot high wind
barrier surrounding the back of her house. Annual rainfall was min-
imal and the cattle crop was dependent on rain that rarely came.
When it did rain, everything looked up smiling in celebration. The
air would be charged as flashes of lightening cracked out of the dis-
tant clouds and gusts of wind announced the coming refreshing. A
cowboy could smell the high, fresh, ion charged air for miles before
the spout finally opened on the thirsty land. As children there was
a particularly happy reveling brought about by the rain. Every

effort was made to get out in the middle of it while it poured down. Dry roads, dusty and rutted, were transformed into a playground of thick red mud as the moisture pooled and mixed with the dust. Before long, the children were painted head to toe like some aboriginal army of pygmies dancing about in giggling foolishness akin to Gene Kelly in the old movie classic "Singing in the Rain." It was a joyous time of renewal for the earth as much as it was necessary for survival.

When Zechariah said, "Ask the Lord for rain in the time of the latter rain," he referred to one of the most joyous celebrations of the Jewish faith. Sukkot is the holiest and grandest of the Hebrew feasts. Also called the Feast of Tabernacles, it is one of the three appointed feasts wherein all Israel was to appear before the Lord. "On the fifteenth of the seventh month is the Feast of Tabernacles for seven days to Yahweh. On the first day is a solemn assembly; you shall do no laborious work of any kind...You shall dwell in tabernacles for seven days."[1] The rejoicing community includes everyone – family, servants, orphans, widows, Levites and sojourners. In ancient times each participant would prepare for the week-long feast by collecting branches of myrtle, willow and palm in the area of Jerusalem in order to build a sukkah or temporary booth.[2] These sukkah were joyful reminders of the temporary dwellings built by their forefathers in the wilderness. They symbolize protection, preservation and shelter from heat and storm.[3] Both the psalmist David and the prophet Isaiah speak of the qualities of the tabernacle. Isaiah describes the glory that covers the dwelling places on Mount Zion. He says, "over all the glory there will be a covering."[4] The Hebrew word that he uses for covering is *chuppah,* the canopy used in the Jewish wedding ceremony. While Pentecost follows Passover as a celebration of the engagement of God to His people, the Feast of Tabernacles points to the union of the bride and her groom as He comes to take His wife into their wedding supper. Sukkot indicates the final ingathering of those who serve the Lord. It annually proclaims the second coming of Christ. Sukkot is the most joyous time imaginable. The rejoicing experienced by those who are invited to celebrate the wedding supper and the celebration of the joy of harvest are similar. When the bride and her groom come together in consummation and enjoyment of their covenant love, it is ultimate joy. The bridal chamber gives us a picture of revival as God visits His people and they experience His glory.

Sukkot marked the celebration of the final ingathering of the year. It signified that the latter rains bringing harvest were set to begin. For Jews gathered in Jerusalem Sukkot was a dual celebration. They gave thanks for the ingathering and prayed for the rains to come. In Israel rain is absolutely necessary for life. Rain in Scripture indicates the visitation of God by the Spirit. Rain brings revival, refreshing and restoration. It yields a rich harvest from formerly sown seeds. The prophets used rain as a metaphor of mercy coming down from God in heaven to the inhabitants of the earth. Describing promised restoration Joel prophesied, "Be glad then, you children of Zion, and rejoice in the Lord your God; for He has given you the former rain faithfully, and He will cause the rain to come down to you—the former rain, and the latter rain in the first month."[5] In the aftermath of a devastating plague that had destroyed all of Judah's crops resulting in famine, Joel speaks of the visitation of the Spirit of God. He said their mourning would be replaced with joy and the years of devastation would be recovered in abundance. Joel's audience was desperate for intervention, but the ultimate fulfillment of his prophecy came on the day of Pentecost after the resurrection of Christ. What must the disciples have been thinking those ten days as they tarried? Surely the joy of resurrection had replaced their initial despair at losing their Lord. Now they waited for something unknown. Huddled together remembering the terrible scenes of the crucifixion, remembering their wonderment at the resurrection of their Savior in whom they hoped, their hearts must have longed for the presence of the One they loved. When the Spirit rain came, their mourning turned to joy. The outpouring not only caused rejoicing, sinners repented! Repentance brought the times of refreshing the Lord had promised. The witnesses who drank in these refreshing waters became inebriated with God's presence. The water and wine poured out on the altar of tarrying prayer produced salvation among many souls. In every place rain is mentioned in Scripture, the end result is food. Revival is refreshing, new life, deliverance, harvest, restoration, promise and rejoicing.

The rejoicing that revival produces refreshes the languishing soul. But God has a determined purpose in sending His joy. In God's economy, "the joy of the Lord is my strength."[6] Revival brings joy and strengthens those who receive it. The harvest season is labor intensive. Before the feast laborers work long hours day and night bringing in the crops. On the other hand, when the harvest fails, Habakkuk says, "I will still rejoice in the Lord, I will joy in the God of my salvation. The Lord God is my strength."[7] So we see in times of abundance and in times of famine, our strength comes from the joy of God's presence.

Chariots of Fire is the wonderful story of a Scottish missionary to China named Eric Liddle. As a young man, Liddle was an Olympic track champion. In the movie, he tells his family, "I know that God has made me for a purpose. But He has also made me fast and when I run, I feel His pleasure!" The joy of the Lord infused Liddle with the strength that made him a champion. The nations watched as he won the gold medal for England. In the same way, heaven watched as Eric sprinted over eternity's finish line. In the words of the apostle, the young man "finished the course and fought the good fight" as a minister of the gospel. Eric Liddle gave his life on the mission field.

Feast of Tabernacles was the most joyous of all celebrations. A noisy, holy entourage including fire-juggling priests and throngs of ecstatic worshipers went from the Temple down to the pool of Siloam. There the High Priest filled a golden pitcher with water from the "wells of salvation." The procession wound back to the Temple through the Water Gate. Accompanied by thousands who danced tumultuously and sang the psalms, the priest bore this living water back to the altar. Ascending the broad Southern steps, the Levites chanted, 'Our feet are standing within thy gates, O Jerusalem." Trumpets blaring, the priest poured water and wine over the altar. The wine signified inebriation from God's presence. Water and wine meant double rejoicing for God's people. This especially clamorous celebration marked the pinnacle of the Feast. The sages say, "Whoever did not see the rejoicing of the water drawing ceremony had never seen rejoicing in his lifetime."[8] During this ceremony of double rejoicing Jesus made His declaration recorded in the gospel of John. "In the last day, that great day of the feast, Jesus stood and cried out, saying, 'If anyone thirsts, let him come to Me and drink. He who believes on Me, as the Scripture has said, out of his heart will flow rivers of living water!"[9] The Son of God was saying in the clearest possible way that He alone was the source of life and blessing; that He could meet every need of every human heart; that He is the High Priest of mankind and that He has opened the well of salvation for all to joyfully draw. The Hebrew sages also teach that the shekinah Presence and the spirit of prophecy are drawn down upon the believer through joy. They say the glory and the voice of the Lord elude those with unhappy hearts.[10] This is the longing that Jesus is answering when He shouts out on the final day of the feast that He is the source of Living water. John points out that the Living water, *mayim chayim*, is the Holy Spirit.

The Holy Spirit is the primary figure in revival! The water libation performed during Sukkot was the segue between the culmination of one harvest and the preparation for the next. As the priestly processional brought those waters from Siloam to the altar, they sang the words of joyful visitation from Isaiah chapter 12:

And in that day you will say:

"O Lord, I will praise You;

Though you were angry with me,

Your anger is turned away, and You comfort me.

Behold, God is my salvation,

I will trust and not be afraid;

"For Yah, the Lord, is my strength and song;

He also has become my salvation."

Therefore with joy you will draw water

From the wells of salvation.

And in that day you will say:

"Praise the Lord, call upon His name;

Declare His deeds among the peoples,

Make mention that His name is exalted.

Sing to the Lord,

For He has done excellent things;

This is known in all the earth.

Cry out and shout, O inhabitants of Zion,

For great is the Holy One of Israel in your midst!"

This is the perfect hymn to the Holy Spirit. The Holy Spirit is the principle purveyor of the kingdom of God. He is the messenger of visitation, revival and salvation. His name is Comforter. He is the one who empowers every vessel who receives Him. As we have seen, the work of the Holy Spirit is essential in salvation. Revival brings salvation.

In revival judgment is turned back and God's hand is made evident. Hosea describes this when He called his people to repentance, "Come, and let us return to the Lord; For He has torn, but He will heal us; He has stricken, but He will bind us up...He will come to us like the rain, like the latter and former rains to the earth."[11] Now we understand better the prophecy about the great revival that came on the day of Pentecost. The most significant manifestation of that day in the upper room was the fruit. As that small gathering of 120 persons began to rejoice in the Holy Spirit, they confessed with their mouths in other tongues the "wonderful works of God."[12] Thousands came to salvation as the rivers of living water came pouring out of these newly filled vessels! This is a principle of revival visitation.

The Holy Spirit brings rejoicing and salvation! As the water and wine of the living waters ceremony overflowed the altar, they ultimately returned to the 'salt sea' in fulfillment of Ezekiel's vision of the River that would heal the nations. It is also what Zechariah prophesies when he says, "In that day a fountain shall be opened...for sin and for uncleaness."[13] The libation of living waters poured out on the altar on Simcha Torah, the day of rejoicing, is like the latter rain of revival visiting the earth to quench the thirst for life in everyone who comes in preparation for Christ's appearing. The pool of Siloam from which the feast waters are drawn is mentioned in the account of Jesus' healing of the blind man on the steps of the Temple in John 9:6-7. He spat on the ground and made clay. Jesus rubbed clay on the eyes of the man blind from birth and sent him to wash in Siloam at the bottom of the stairs. When the man washed he could see! This pool is also mentioned in the rebuilding of Jerusalem and the repairing of her walls under the ministries of Ezra and Nehemiah. The actual site of the pool had not been uncovered until archeologists announced their discovery just before the Feast of Tabernacles in 2005! The timing and the significance of this discovery is prophetic. Finding Siloam at the very time of year the ancients rejoiced in the water drawing ceremony is no coincidence. The Holy Spirit is indicating He is coming in fresh Pentecost. The discovery of the pool exactly as John described it validates the theology of the Holy Spirit as the Helper of all believers. Certain scholars considered John's gospel to be invented fables until Siloam was uncovered. Once again, the 'stories' of the Bible are proving to be real historical events. Hidden for thousands of years, the discovery of this ancient pool is a sign to Israel and to all who long for Messiah's appearing. The discovery of Siloam speaks to us again that blind eyes are being opened as the miracles of God are restored to this generation. Living waters of joyous revival are washing the bride of God and preparing her for His coming. Like the 100 year bloom and ancient Siloam seeds of promise that have been hidden in the dust of many generations are making their appearance. These signs announce that He is coming. Prepare for harvest! Joyous revival is on the way.

The believer's KEY to living in joyous revival is to ACCENTUATE THE POSITIVE: As the ancients pointed out, the happy heart draws down the presence of God. Focus on the fruit. Enter into the joy. Take time to smell the flowers! "So I looked for You in the sanctuary to see Your power and Your glory." Psalm 63:2

---

[1] Leviticus 23:24-42

[2] Nehemiah 8:13-18

[3] Leviticus 23:40-41; Deuteronomy 16:14

[4] Isaiah 4:5

[5] Joel 2:23

[6] Nehemiah 8:10

[7] Habakkuk 3:18

[8] Talmud: Sukkah 5:1

[9] John 7:37-38

[10] Babylonian Talmud: 30b; Jerusalem Talmud: Sukkah 5:1

[11] Hosea 6:1-3

[12] Acts 2:11

13 Zechariah 13:1

CHAPTER SEVEN

First Responders in Revival

Every season of fresh rain from heaven brings revival and refreshing to a generation. Historically the move of the Spirit often began with women. Since the birth of the church at Pentecost, women have been first responders to the "promise of the Father." Joel prophesied, "I will pour out my Spirit on all flesh."[1] Throughout Scripture, women have had a special history in the visitations of God. Through these visitations, God has been testifying of something better for women than the yoke of subjugation Eve received as penalty for sin in the Garden. From Miriam to Deborah, Esther to Ruth and the many women of the New Testament, the "firsts" when God moves have been women. Women have always been God's *first responders!*

A hallmark of true revival is the restoration of women's lives in their personal sphere, acceptance into ministry and authority in public leadership. History is filled with the testimony of great women arising during revival. Burning bright by the light of His anointing oil, time and again, God's women arise in the power of the Spirit. Particularly during periods of cultural darkness and social duress, women of God come to the forefront. Joan of Arc, Florence Nightingale, Harriet Tubman, Susan B. Anthony and the friends among the Quakers were lights shining brightly during the darkest nights of history. Anointed by the Holy Spirit, they provoked and established social justice, healing, reconciliation and salvation for many. The torchbearers who caught the flames of Azusa and carried the light to China through missions included many women. In Jesus' earthly life and ministry and in the unfolding early church era, women were used of the Holy Spirit equally to men. The first miracle Jesus did was at the behest of a woman. At the wedding in Cana, His mother compelled God to do His unusual act. The first Gentile Jesus sought out was a woman at a well. The first to speak with Jesus after His resurrection and give witness to that important event was a woman. The resurrection was the singular event sealing, confirming and initiating the great salvation Jesus proclaimed. Jesus "appeared first" to Mary Magdalene, out of whom He had cast seven demons! She became a sent one, apostle to the apostles. Jesus' commission of a woman as an eyewitness to establish His testimony was a blatant contradiction to the culture of the day. Paul writes, Jesus was, "declared to be the Son of God with power according to the Spirit of holiness, by the resurrection from the dead."[2] Jesus ordained this definitive message to be witnessed to by women first! He did not wait for the arrival of his male disciples. Rather, He sent faithful women to deliver the message that He was risen from the dead. This first recorded act as the resurrected Lord, confirmed that God considers women viable messengers of His liable proofs.

This incident may seem coincidental, but in the cultural context of the day, Jesus was proclaiming a message about the redemption of women and his inclusion of them in ministry. Women were not accorded status as legal witness in the court of law. Only men were accepted for testimonial establishment of truth concerning a legal matter. Sending women as His personal eye-witnesses of the resurrection meant God had planted the standard for a new order, firmly embracing women as central participants in spiritual matters and full partners in unfolding salvation history. The Risen Savior challenged an age-old prejudice that women were incapable of recognizing truth and carrying the message of God. If Jesus had meant for culture to retain this tradition of holding women as second-class citizens without authority or voice in His kingdom, He would have remained at the tomb until the men arrived. With the proof that He had risen, Jesus let it be known that the curse of Eve was finally broken! It was an object lesson for the rest of His disciples. Mark says, "when they heard that He was alive and had been seen by her, they did not believe." Luke says that the report of the women who went in the tomb and spoke with angels "seemed like idle tales and they did not believe them." Jesus rebuked those men that did not believe the women's report. He demonstrated the fulfillment of Isaiah's words depicting Jerusalem's glorious revival: "And in that day seven women shall take hold of one man, saying: 'We will eat our own food and wear our own apparel; only let us be called by your name, to take away our reproach.' In that day the Branch of the LORD shall be beautiful and glorious; And the fruit of the earth shall be excellent and appealing for those of Israel who have escaped. And it shall come to pass that he who is left in Zion and remains in Jerusalem will be called holy—everyone who is recorded among the living in Jerusalem."[3] The Branch has taken away the reproach of woman and restored her through His body and blood. Furthermore, He is preparing Himself an eternal helpmate, the bride of Christ, made up of women as well as men.

The inclusion of women in spiritual service through the infilling of the Holy Spirit is a significant pattern of church history. Women arose as house church leaders and worked in positions of influence and leadership during the first two centuries of Christianity. This is in stark contrast with the traditions and restrictions that evolved as the Church became more and more politicized and formalized. But the Lord who is Spirit has ordained women for liberty. In *The Rise of Christianity,* sociologist Rodney Stark writes, "Amidst contemporary denunciations of Christianity as patriarchal and sexist, it is easily forgotten that the early church was so especially attractive to women that in 370 the emperor Valentinian issued a written order to Pope Damasus I requiring that Christian missionaries cease calling at the homes of pagan women."[4] Stark goes on to show that in the midst of a society where women were devalued to the level of property, where infant girls were left to die in the sewers, where husbands were not compelled to be faithful, where the least suspicion of infidelity gave men power to divorce his wife, and abortion was rampant, the teachings of Christ liberated women. This good news for women was a primary factor in the growth of the early church. Not only were women drawn to Christianity in great numbers because they were given value in their roles as wives and mothers, but they were integral players in the leadership of the early church.

The "good news" brought forth liberty to every area of women's lives: past, present and eternal future! Elevation of women was the inevitable fruit of the culture of life commanded through the gospel message. It drew women in great numbers to the early faith. The kingdom of God is like no kingdom on earth. In this kingdom where Jesus reigns, women are received and valued alongside men; both partners in a marriage are expected to fulfill their vows and respect one another and monogamy is required of all who aspire to leadership. These principles elevate the value of a woman as a wife. Many sacral heathen practices devalue children born of women. Christianity forbids abortion, a grisly and widely practiced custom in cultures then and now. In the kingdom of Christ, girl babies are of equal value to boy infants. The faith makes women equal inheritors and valued influencers.

Jesus' life and ministry showed that He received and valued women without any prejudice. In the home of Lazarus, Rabbi Jesus makes another statement that refutes traditional exclusion of women from spiritual instruction. From the time of Moses, due to their demanding roles in the home, women were exempted from much of the requirements and obligations of the Law. However, what began as a pragmatic solution for women burdened with the responsibilities of raising and caring for a family, had developed into a doctrine that prohibited women from participating freely in worship and the study of the Law. In the story of Mary and Martha,

Jesus is making another pointed contradiction to the traditions regarding women. In Luke's account, Mary is described as "sitting at Jesus' feet." This term is the reference for men being tutored in the Word of God by a Rabbi. Martha complained as would be expected since her sister was neglecting the woman's appointed place according to Judaic custom. But Jesus said, "Mary has chosen the better part which will not be taken away from her."[5] This astounding remark by the King of heaven indicates women have wider and higher spiritual destiny than domestic responsibilities alone. Being a disciple of the Word is a women's portion. Spiritual mentoring is a "better part" of her inheritance. One that Jesus will not deny her!

Scenes from the Court of Women during the time of Jesus' earthly ministry illustrate a pattern for the coming revival and the role that women will take in the final ingathering of the harvest. Of Jesus' ministry recorded in Jerusalem, most of His teaching took place in the Court of Women where His female disciples were able to sit around Him without restriction. An addition to the original layout of the Tabernacle and Temple, this court was added by Herod in the construction of the Second Temple. Although so named, this area was not exclusive to women, however, it was the only section of the Temple complex where ritually purified women were allowed to worship, learn and pray. Beyond this court, at its western boundary, the thick, high, 'middle wall of partition' separated all but ritually pure Jewish men and priests from the Holy Place and altar area of sacrifice. Diseased persons, those with physical defects, slaves, women and Gentiles were all forbidden to approach God beyond the Court of Women. Stone markers warned of the death penalty for violators of this law. The Court was the center of activity for various rituals and administrative aspects of Temple upkeep. One of the most significant and joyous of these occasions centered around Sukkot or the Feast of Tabernacles – one of God's appointed Feasts that points to revival, the final ingathering of the harvest and ultimately, to the wedding of the Bridegroom to His bride.

The climax of every Sukkot celebration was the ceremony of the water libation. The Court of Women served as the central gathering place as ecstatic revelers worshiped in joy and thanksgiving for the rain of His shekinah presence while the priest poured the living water out of the golden pitcher on the altar. Up fifteen steps from the Court of Women the Levites, their instruments in hand, ascended to the glorious court above. Singing as they went into the place women could not, ancient priests worshiped with words from David's Psalms of Ascent during the great harvest festival of Sukkot.[6] "When the Lord brought back the captivity of Zion, we were like those who dream. Then our mouths were filled with laughter and our tongues with joyful singing. Then they said among the nations, the Lord has done great things for us." Every Feast, the Court of Women was filled with light. As part of the celebration, which lasted all through the night, huge menorahs filled with oil were set up in the Court of Women. Their wicks were worn liturgical garments, and young priests in training ascended ladders to fill the bowls of the lamps, which could be up to eighty feet tall.[7] So magnificent was the light that streamed from the Court of Women during the Feast of Tabernacles that Jerusalem was given the name, "a city set on a hill." The sages say that the light shone in the doorway of every house in Jerusalem.[8] This is the probable background for Jesus' statement: "I am the light of the world."[9]

The culmination of the Sukkot celebrations was the most joyous of all processionals: the drawing down of water. A noisy, holy entourage that included fire-juggling priests and thousands of ecstatic worshipers descended down to the Pool of Siloam. A great parade followed the priests and singers to draw water from this "well of salvation." The procession wound its way back up into the Temple where the water was poured out on the altar together with wine. At that point, the two great doors in the middle wall were opened. Peering into the altar area where only men and priests could ascend, were women, slaves and the disabled. Religious leaders during the era of Herod's temple became concerned that liberty and rejoicing by men and women mixing together during the water-drawing ceremony led to 'too much levity.' Fearing that men and women mingling in the feast processions and court led to sin, a balcony was constructed over the Court of Women in order to separate women from the men during the Sukkot. According to the Mishnah, *'the rectification,'* as it was called, was a solution to the possibility that a woman's presence in the court with men might lead to lewdness.[10] From there, no longer able to partici-pate, women observed the great celebration of God. Synagogues followed suit, putting females behind screens. This separation reinforced customs that already considered a woman's voice, hair, form, presence and ultimately her influence akin to sin! The female gender became condemned as an unholy distraction. Sight and sound of her diminished from public influence and spiritual service in those institutions and all they influenced.

Jewish historian Josephus records the great *Nicanor* doors in the middle wall of partition refused to stay closed after the resur-rection. During the night watches the great doors into the Holy Place would open on their own. It was as if God was giving a sign to all that Joel's prophecy had come to pass. Jew and Gentile, slave and free, men and women, anyone who thirsts could enter as equal inheritors of the covenant. The Holy Place formerly only admitted Jewish men without bodily defect and priests.

While the first few centuries of the church adhered to Jesus' teaching and broke with the traditional exclusion of women, as the visitation of the Holy Spirit receded, prejudices resurfaced and began to shape the face of the Church and her doctrine concerning women that we know today. Early church fathers shrouded women with cultural and religious prohibitions stemming from gender prejudice. Even the injunctions against women found in Islamic sharia law are suspiciously similar to extremes of ancient Judeo-

Christian culture prominent in the time of Mohammed. But a new rectification is under way! The Creator, who from the Beginning made them in His image both male and female, is the Lord of Harvest. The Holy Spirit is filling their bowls with oil and making daughters His co-laborers in the harvest.

Christ is the Supreme Champion of women and all that concerns them. On the final day of the Feast, Jesus stood at the altar, the doors in the wall of partition open for all to hear and see and announced a new and living way for the nations to be reconciled to God: "If anyone thirsts, let him come to Me and drink. He who believes in Me, as the Scripture has said, out of his heart will flow rivers of living water."[11] His statement was for all those who believed, including the ones who were excluded as outside observers. We are all invited to drink. God makes women joint heirs through His blood by the Holy Spirit. He made them in His own image and is conforming them to His glory in these days. The outpouring of the Holy Spirit sanctifies, anoints, equips and commissions women for spiritual service. Not only is the women's court being filled with the light of God, the oil of the Spirit is empowering men and women for service. The Holy Spirit of God is making daughters co-laborers in the harvest. As the night of old Jerusalem was dispelled by the lights erected in the women's court, God is anointing and raising up women to lift the lamp of His coming and light the way for many to be reconciled to Him. Their light is breaking upon the dark door of every home. Devastated lives, ruined cities and impoverished nations around the world in the 21st century are hearing the voice of godly women as well as godly men. Their song arises in the night as praises to God declaring Christ's Jubilee has come in the eternal blood of His salvation covenant. We hear their voice. We have begun to see the lovely face of holy women, reflecting the Bridegroom, leading in His Name.

As the day of the heavenly Bridegroom draws near, women light-bearers will be more prominent than at any other time in history. A new day, spoken by the prophets and demonstrated by Christ is here! The universe is about to witness the unveiling of the bride of Christ, and we shall see women in the church arise and shine as never before. Their light has come. A pageant of triumph of new first responders is the testimony of godly women accepting their inheritance. As Song of Songs says, "The winter is over and gone...flowers appear on the earth." As the end of the age draws near the Lord of Harvest is calling women to the fields white with souls. Grain in the fields has come to a full head. He is calling forth reapers. Women of the Spirit, ministers of grace, messengers of fire, rush to bring restoration and redemption out of the treasuries of His kingdom, joining anointed men to do the works of Christ and the greater works. Ready with the gifts of the Spirit, women are going forth as His witness to the Resurrection again. The Church looks up; her redemption draws near, a virtuous wife she strengthens her arms to rebuild devastation wrought by storms of the enemy. The Bride prepares to reign and rule with Him for eternity.

The believer's KEY to receiving the first responders in revival is RECOGNIZING THE ANOINTING: When you welcome the Holy Spirit honor the vessel who brings Him, be they young or old, male or female, rich or poor. Jesus wept over Jerusalem because her priests did not recognize that He was the one they had been waiting for. "Your house will be desolate and you shall see Me no more until you say, 'Blessed is he, (or she) who comes in the name of the Lord.'" Matthew 23:39

---

[1] Joel 2:28

[2] Romans 1:4.

[3] Isaiah 4:1-3

4 Rodney Stark, *The Rise of Christianity*, 95

5 Luke 10:42

6 Psalms 120 - 134

7 Talmud: Sukkah 5:3

8 Ibid.

9 John 8:12

10 Talmud Sukka 5,2

11 John 7:37-38

CHAPTER EIGHT

Revival is Rewarding

We were almost home. I was in revival when He asked the sixth time, 'What is it about revival?' By this time, I wasn't asking back, just waiting as His answer came, 'It's rewarding!' I could feel the favor of the King of heaven on all those who were willing to embrace this messy, spontaneous, costly, glorious, joyous, rewarding revival. I considered the pearl of great price and how the man who purchased that field knew the treasure hidden in it was more valuable than all that it could cost him. Only a fool would miss such an investment opportunity! I girded myself up and made a choice to take that tiny step, a step into His glory at the throne without ever leaving home.

The rich covenant that we possess as Christians began with the faith of one man thousands of years ago. After Abram had risked all to rescue an insincere nephew, the king of Salem met him in the gates of Jerusalem. The exchange that followed reveals the fabric of the father of our faith.

"Then Melchizedek king of Salem brought out bread and wine; he was the priest of God Most High. And he blessed him and said: 'Blessed be Abram of God Most High, possessor of heaven and earth; and blessed be God Most High, who has delivered your enemies into your hand.' And he gave him a tithe of all. Now the king of Sodom said to Abram, 'Give me the persons, and take the goods for yourself.' But Abram said to the king of Sodom, 'I have raised my hand to the Lord, God Most High, the possessor of heaven and earth, that I will take nothing, from a thread to a sandal strap, and that I will not take anything that is yours, lest you should say, 'I have made Abram rich...' Gen 14:18-23

After this, God appears to Abram in a vision and tells him, "I am your shield and exceedingly great reward."[1] In another place, the Bible says, those who come to God must believe that He is and that He is a rewarder of those who diligently seek him. The rewards of faith are many, tangible and nontagible. They are rewards a believer possesses now and will yet inherit in the eternal kingdom. A Christian's life can never be determined according to natural circumstances or immediate satisfaction. The rewards of faith are ultimately spiritual. But the faithful can be assured, like Abraham, a personal encounter with the living God is inevitable. John saw God in like manner to Abram. Jesus stood before John and made this promise, "Behold I am coming soon. My reward is with me and I will give to everyone according to what he has done."[2]

One of the greatest rewards of living in revival is seeing the next generation encounter God. When God told Abram He was his rewarder, Abram said, "You have given me no children." Solomon, the son of David who experienced the glory of visitation face to face in the Temple he built, said this in his psalm of ascent, " Except the Lord build the house, they labor in vain that build it...it is vain for your to rise up early, to sit up late, to eat the bread of sorrows... Behold children are an inheritance: and the fruit of the womb is His reward."[3] Solomon possessed and fully imbibed every experience and riches the earth presented. He also stood bodily in the very presence of the fiery cloud of God that filled the temple He built. In all of that, Solomon, like Abraham, pointed to the reward of God that is greatest: children, a next generation, who know their God and serve Him.

This is the true nature of spiritual revival sent by God. While He ordains the present generation to be revived in order to flourish, to be enriched and to rejoice, God intends that revival produce living

seeds. Seed assures Him the visitation will not end in that generation, but shall also bear an even more glorious harvest in the next.
This understanding has been lacking in many revivals in the past.
We see it perhaps most painfully clear in those who received the
most recent rivers of refreshing. For nearly a decade, in the late
1990's much of the Western world was touched by the overflow of
contemporary revival. With great emphasis on things of personal
refreshing, renewal, the Father's love and a new light-hearted experience of God, the revelers typically became self-focused. Sadly,
like many revivals of the past, even this latest outpouring waned
with first generation experience. The great river of life Ezekiel saw
pouring out from under the throne also contains a mystery. A mystery easily understood. "So shall it be wherever the river flows
everything will live. Fisherman will stand along the shore spreading nets. The fish will be of many kinds, like the fish of the great
sea. But the swamps and marshes will not be made fresh, they will
be left for salt."4 What do we notice about the river of life, even
life flowing out of the throne of God himself? We note that even
God-life by the Spirit will stagnate and die when it flows into a
reservoir that feeds nothing. A generation longing for revival with
no conscious determination that what they receive is to feed a new
crop, will ultimately become swamps and marshes. Theirs will be a
memory of the days when fisherman spread their nets and many
people came out of the river, but it will only be a study of history.
"Children are an inheritance of the Lord: the fruit of the womb His
reward." Biblical revival is the spiritual entrance of the manifest
presence of God intimately communing with man corporately and
individually. Like intimacy of the marriage bed, God intends
revival to produce fruit. The Lord of life is seeking His reward, the
'fruit of the woman.'

"Fruit trees of all kinds will grow on both banks of the river.
Their leaves will not wither, nor will their fruit fail. Every month
they will bear because the water from the sanctuary flows to them.
Their fruit will serve for food and their leaves for healing of the

nations."[5] The life of God, making entrance through revival produces rewards on three levels. The psalmist describes the man dwelling in the perpetual Presence, "He is like a tree planted by streams of water, which yields its fruit in season and whose leaf does not wither. Whatever he does prospers."[6] Those who drink from the river of revival are trees planted by the Lord. Their root goes down deep and their branches become a shelter for many, including a generation to come through the seed-bearing fruit they produce. The revival streams they draw in produces in them fruit for eating and feeds their contemporaries with the experience of God. The seed of that fruit falls in the soil of men's hearts and the influence of it will inspire a young generation into revival as well. All the while, the presence and influence, the leaves, of the revival generation will contain signs and wonders that will be healing and salvation for nations. This is true revival.

Jesus said, "Unless a corn of wheat falls to the ground and dies it remains alone."[7] So it is with a generation, a church or a person who receives revival only with the intention of self-fulfillment. The living thing becomes a swamp. Conversely, if they intend to sow themselves for the sake of the kernel of life within, death to self assures a next generation. Like the corn of wheat they will bear much fruit. This mortal body, the deeds of the flesh, in fact, this temporary life in the flesh itself can be likened to the chaff encasing the kernel of wheat. A Christian's willingness to sacrifice the chaff for the sake of the life in the kernel assures revival in the next generation and is in itself a great reward. Jesus said, "The kingdom of heaven is like yeast that a woman took and mixed into a large amount of flour until it worked through all the dough."[8] Jesus gave two other parables that illustrate the man who receives revival. He said, "The kingdom of heaven is like treasure hidden in a field, which a man found and hid; and for joy over it he goes and sells all that he has and buys that field." He continues, "Again the kingdom of heaven is like a merchant seeking beautiful pearls, who, when he found one pearl of great price, went and sold all that he had and bought it."[9] The men in these parables remind us of Abram and of Solomon. Their faith and wisdom serve as a compass for receiving revival and passing it on to the next generation. Paul the apostle said, "We have this treasure in earthen vessels....So then death is working in us, but life in you...therefore we make it our aim, whether present or absent to be well-pleasing to Him. For if we are beside ourselves it is for God, or if we are of sound mind it is for you. For the love of Christ compels us."[10]

Procopius is identified by the early church fathers as the 'first of the martyrs.' As the early church advanced and threatened the Roman empire, representatives of Rome set to snuff out the lamp of Christian revival fire. A bishop in Palestine, Procopius was ordered to offer pagan libations honoring four emperors as gods. He refused and was immediately beheaded. Other bishops were seized and Eusebius reported that they were, "scourged with innumerable strokes of the lash, racked in their limbs, and gauled in their sides with torturing instruments, some with intolerable fetters by which the joints of their hands were dislocated. Nevertheless, they bore the event."[11] In another place, he tells of Romanus, who was seized at Antioch: "he was to die by flames, with a cheerful countenance and a most ardent mind, he received the sentence and was led away. He was then tied to the stake, and when the wood was heaped up about him... waiting the word from the expected emperor, he exclaimed, 'where then is the fire?'" Romanus was dragged back before the emperor who had his tongue cut out."[12] Valentina of the faithful seized in Gaza was subjected to incredible cruelties before Governor Maximinus. Watching another Christian woman undergo torture, Valentina exclaimed, "How long then will you thus cruelly torture my sister?" Ordered seized by Maximinus, Valentina was dragged to the altar by force, she kicked it over together with its fire, inciting the rage, they seized upon her and did worse than before."[13] What inspired such joy and commitment?

Sociologist Rodney Stark asks this question of the early Christian faith, "How could any rational person make sacrifices on behalf of unseen supernatural entities?" In his book, the *Rise of Christianity*, Stark says, "when analyzed properly, religious sacrifices and stigmas – even when acute cases are considered – usually turn out to represent rational choices. Indeed, the more that people must sacrifice for their faith, the greater the value of the rewards they gain in return." Stark says, "When applied to early Christianity, these propositions yield the conclusion that sacrifice and stigma were the dynamo behind the rise of Christianity... For the fact is that Christianity was by far the best religious 'bargain' around."[14] In Stark's words, *"religion supplies compensators for rewards that are scarce or unavailable."* Most people desire immortality, therefore, "Martyrs are the most credible exponents of a value of a religion, and this is especially true if there is a voluntary aspect to their martyrdom...Costly demands strengthen a religious group by mitigating, 'free-rider' problems that otherwise lead to low levels of member commitment and participation....High costs tend to screen out potential members whose commitment and participation would otherwise be low."[15] The Apocryphal account of the gospel of Peter relates the account of his martyrdom. Initially the saints are able to persuade the apostle to leave Rome in lieu of his pending arrest and execution. The story goes that as Peter was exiting the gates of the city, he met the Lord coming in. Surprised, Peter asked, "where are you going?" And the Lord replied, "I'm going to be crucified." Whereupon the apostle said, "But Lord, can you be crucified again?" To which Jesus answered, "Yes." Peter turned about and went to his death by crucifixion. Perhaps Ignatius explains it best when he wrote to the believers in Rome who were interceding to gain him pardon from execution, "I am afraid your love will do me wrong, for you of course, it is easy to achieve your object; but for me it is difficult to win my way to God.... Grant me no more than that you let my blood be spilled in sacrifice.... I am writing to all the Churches and state emphatically to all that I die willingly...I beg you, do not show me unseasonable kindness. Suffer me to be the food of wild beasts...God's wheat I am, and by the teeth of wild beasts I am to be ground, that I may prove Christ's pure bread."[16] Tertullian once said, "The blood of the martyrs is the seed of the Christians." In his day, Christianity was largely free of persons who wanted to reap the benefits of religion without sharing in the sacrifices and commitments. Perhaps we could say that during the first centuries of Christianity there was more wheat than chaff.

Going back to the 100 year bloom and Azusa, we remember the characteristic hull of desert seeds. Their 'thick wax-like coating' preserved the living seed until the rains came. We think of previous lives so rubbed with the anointing oil of God that even their bones, like Elisha's though long buried, resurrected any dead thing that touched them. It behooves us then, in a revival generation to be so saturated with the anointing of His presence that the life in us, while we die to the flesh of self, may assure successive revival in generations after us.

Thinking of the inability of the rich young ruler to divest himself of the 'chaff' of his riches, we read in Tertullian's accounts that the revival of early Christianity inspired willing liberality, "not taken thence and spent on feasts and drinking bouts, and eating houses, but to support and bury the poor, to supply the wants of boys and girls destitute of means and parents, and of old persons confined to the house; such too as have suffered shipwreck; and if there happen to be any in the minds, or banished to the islands, or shut up in the prisons for nothing but their fidelity to the cause of God's Church, they become nurselings of their confession.." C.S. Lewis said, "We must not be troubled by unbelievers when they say this promise of a reward makes the Christian life a mercenary affair. There are different kinds of rewards. There is the reward that has no natural connection to the things you do to earn it and is quite foreign to the desires that ought to accompany those things." Lewis spoke of the reward of love in this way, "marriage is the proper desire for a real lover, and he is not mercenary for desiring it. A general who fights well in order to get a peerage is mercenary. A general who fights for victory is not, victory being the proper reward of battle as marriage is the proper reward of love. The proper rewards are not simply tacked on to the activity for which they are given, but are the activity itself in consummation." Lewis also said, "If we are made for heaven the desire for our proper place will already be in us, but not yet attached to the true object, and will even appear as the rival of that object... if a trans-temporal, trans-finite good is our real destiny, then any other good on which our desire fixes must be in some degree fallacious, must bear at best only a symbolical relation to what will truly satisfy."

In his famous sermon, "Weight of Glory," C.S. Lewis proposed, "If you ask twenty good men today what they thought the highest virtues, nineteen would reply unselfishness. But if you had asked almost any of the great Christians of old he would have replied love. You see what has happened?" Lewis asks. "A negative term has been substituted for a positive... the negative idea of unselfishness carries the suggestion not primarily of securing good things for others, but of going without them ourselves." Lewis goes on "I do not think this is the Christian virtue of love. The New Testament has a lot to say about self-denial, but not about self-denial as an end in itself. We are told to deny ourselves and to take up our crosses in order that we may follow Christ, and nearly every description of what we shall ultimately find if we do so contains an appeal to desire." Lewis suggests that the tendency of modern minds to think that desiring our own good and hoping for enjoyment of it is a bad thing has crept in from the likes of Kant and the stoics. Lewis says, the "unblushing promises of reward and the staggering nature of the rewards promised in the gospels" seems to indicate Jesus finds our "desires not too strong, but too weak. We are half-hearted creatures fooling about with drink and sex and ambition when infinite joy is offered us, like an ignorant child who wants to go on making mud-pies in a slum because he cannot imagine what is meant by the offer of a holiday at the sea. We are far too easily pleased."

The Mishnah *C* records the Jewish sage Antigonus of Socho receiving this admonition from Simeon the Just, "Be not like slaves who serve their master for the sake of the compensation; be like such servants as labor for their master without reward; and let the fear of heaven be upon you." Better yet, let the *reward* of heaven be upon us.

Interviewed by *Christianity Today*, Rodney Stark was asked, *Many churches are lowering the bar to make religion more popular. How would you analyze their efforts?* Stark replied, "They're death wishes. People value religion on the basis of cost, and they don't value the cheapest ones the most. Religions that ask nothing get nothing. You've got a choice: you can be a church or a country club. If you're going to be a church, you'd better offer religion on Sunday. If you're not, you'd better build a golf-course, because you're not going to get away with being a country club with no golf course. If religion gets too cheap, nobody pays the price."

The famous English playwright William Shakespeare had an uncanny gift of portraying human nature. In *The Merchant of Venice* he studies the redemptive power of sacrifice in the contrasts between law and mercy, revenge and forgiveness. A theme in Shakespeare is the struggle to fulfill one's solemn vows when the cost of them comes to bear on the frail human nature of man.

In that play, young Bassanio woos Portia. Other suitors have tried and failed to pass the test devised by the maiden's father. Bassanio is presented three boxes, two ornate of beautiful gold and silver, and one of simple lead. Each box contains something but only one has the image of his love inside. If Bassanio chooses the box containing the portrait of the bride, Portia and her estate will belong to him. As he ponders each box, Bassanio makes an excellent speech of the deceptive nature of our flesh and its like to religious hypocrisy: "So may the outward shows the least themselves the world is still deceived with ornament. In lure would please so tainted and corrupt but being seasoned with a gracious voice obscures the show of evil in religion. What damned error but some sober brow will bless it and approve it with a text; hiding the grossness with fair." Bassanio sees through the lure of external appearance and chooses the simple box. Inside he finds the image of his bride and gains her hand. He does not know that this wife shall soon become a greater treasure of redemption for him than just a good companion.

Before she even weds him, Portia uses her estate to pay a debt owed by Bassanio. Bassanio's true friend, a virtuous man like himself is sentenced to death. Portia's payment purchases Antonio's life. When thanked, Portia replies quickly and freely, "I never did repent of doing good and shall not now. For in companions that do converse and waste the time together there must needs be a like proportion of lineaments of manners and of spirit which makes me think that this Antonio (the friend whose release the bride is purchasing) being the bosom lover of my lord (Bassanio) must needs be like my lord. If it be so how little is the cost I have bestowed in purchasing the semblance of my soul."

Portia saw the image of Bassanio in his friend. She was willing to pay a price to preserve the image of the one she loved. Do you imagine Jesus is being formed in His friends? In your friends? He longs to print His image in many who are marked for death. Would you see in them a "semblance of our soul" and send out treasure to purchase them because of His love?

Within every true worshiper there lies a portrait of the bride Jesus purchased. Like the leaden box Bassanio chose this mystery has been "hidden from ages and generations but now has been revealed to His saints." Paul writes, "God willed to make known what are the riches of the glory of this mystery among the Gentiles." The reward of revival is the revelation of the bride. The face of the eternal lover of the Glorious Man is appearing in our generation. It is worth the sacrifice we make.

The believer's KEY to living in rewarding revival is SACRIFICE: A corn of wheat must fall to the ground and die or else it remains alone. Revival is not primarily for personal experience. The reward of revival is seeing Christ formed in others. Jesus gave everything for this. King David made great sacrifice to bring revival in his generation. "...I will surely buy it for the full price, for I will not take what is yours for the Lord, nor offer burnt offerings with that which costs me nothing." I Chronicles 21:24

---

[1] Genesis 15:1

[2] Revelation 22:12

[3] Psalm 127:1-3 (KJV)

[4] Ezekiel 47:10-11

[5] Ezekiel 47:12

[6] Psalm 1:3

[7] John 12:24

[8] Matthew 13:33 (NIV)

[9] Matthew 13:44-46

[10] 2 Corinthians 4:7,12; 5:9,14.

[11] Eusebius, *The Martyrs of Palestine*, 1850 ed., Chapter 1.

[12] Ibid. Chapter 2

[13] Ibid. Chapter 8

[14] Stark, 167

[15] Ibid., 174, 177

[16] Ignatius, *letter to the Romans*, 1946 ed.

CHAPTER NINE

Pentecost is Primal Revival

"Primal." It even sounds good in the mouth. Primal means the root, the first cause. Primordial implies before the appearance of life on earth, as when the Spirit of God hovered over the wild waste of creation. Primal is the beginning that affects the end. Primal is defined as 'cardinal', serving as an essential component; the fundamental example or argument. Primal means aboriginal; having existed from the beginning; the earliest or original state. Primal is basic and fundamental. The basis of all spirituality is the presence and power of the Holy Spirit. Beginning at the beginning the *rushing* Spirit of God hovered over the wild waste of creation.[1] This is the same Spirit, a rushing, mighty wind, which poured down like fire upon the wild waste of humanity on Pentecost, where He began His unusual act of recreation. As in the beginning, each era of time is a new day unfolding. Blueprints rolled up in His hand, God walks in the garden in the breezy time each evening searching for the man He has made. All around Him creation groans longing to set eyes upon the sons on whom the Spirit rests. Revival is recovery. Visitation from on high is recreation.

Upon the spoken word of God the Spirit rushed to do His unusual act. So it is with revival. Lives lie in waste. Wild beasts of spiritual oppression haunt the dry places until God visits and the Dayspring from on high pours water on the languishing ground. Pentecostal spirituality is on the rise. Out of Azusa, a spiritual fire "roared forth that was to race around the world and touch hundreds of millions of people with its warmth and power...a spiritual hurricane that has already touched nearly half a billion people, and an alternative vision of the human future whose impact may only be in its earliest stages today."[2] Pentecost speaks to "the spiritual emptiness of our time by reaching beyond the levels of creed and ceremony into the core of human religiousness" in that "largely unprocessed nucleus of the psyche in which the unending struggle for a sense of purpose and significance goes on."[3] Are you dry? Are you thirsty? Do you want more of God? Does your church, your city, your family, your nation need a visitation? It's time for revival!

Professor of Divinity at Harvard, Harvey Cox writes about the phenomena of Pentecostal revival in *Fire From Heaven: The Rise of Pentecostal Spirituality and the Reshaping of Religion in the Twenty-first Century*. Cox calls Pentecostal spirituality primal spirituality. Pentecost, described in the second chapter of the Acts of the Apostles, is primal revival: revival at the beginning. No other revival can replace Pentecostal revival. By Cox's description the tongues that rested in flames on each one in Jerusalem is an experience "in which the cognitive grids...that normally prevent people from opening themselves to deeper insights and exultant feelings, are temporarily suspended." Tongue speaking has persisted, he says, because it "represents the core of all Pentecostal conviction: that the Spirit of God needs no mediators but is available to anyone in an intense, immediate, indeed interior way."

Cox says Pentecostal revival recovers the spirituality, speech, piety, and hope of the human race. In this light we see the dramatic impact of the first Pentecost after the resurrection of Christ. He calls the tongue-talking phenomena of Pentecost and Pentecostal revival the "searing realization that the reality of God utterly transcends our puny capacity to describe it...Our corrupt and inadequate language is transformed by God's love into the tongues of angels." Pentecost is primal revival. Revival restores our native tongue and brings the heart to recovery and rest in the Presence of Him who loves us more than all. A German mystic, Jacob Boehme, wrote about the "circular process" present in creation and human nature wherein the end continually seeks the beginning. In the contemporary classic, *The Ancient Language of Eden,* author Don Milam considers that circle: "Man is a wanderer. In the progression of civilization man is inclined to move away from the wonder of the original moment. All of life moves from the simple to the complex. Sometimes this growth is good, sometimes it is bad. It is a tragedy when we migrate from the innocence experienced in the beginning of our relationship with God, drifting toward the complications developed in the process of 'spiritual growth.'"4 How true this is of church history and the advent of visitation as God brings revival. From Pentecost forward we see the attempt of man to complicate the primal moment of the first revival, distancing ourselves in the name of spiritual maturity. Eventually, the vital nature and impact of the initial visitation by God wanes in the affections of the man who received it. Its importance diminishes in the man's soul. Powerful revival is simple and innocent. Primal revival remains fresh as the moment He first appeared.

Milam imagines John about to write his first book. It will tell the story of how John came to know his Beloved Friend, the Lamb who takes away the sins of the whole world. It will carry the seed of that revelation to all future generations. Where to start? What to say first? Milam imagines John sitting at his table, a scribe behind him with quill in hand ready to write down the apostle's words. John thinks back through the years of the growth of the fledgling church. Back through the day the Upper Room was filled with wind and sound. Past the early days of walking with the Lord and back past the day John the Baptizer received the revelation by the river. That was the day the prophet came to know his cousin for the first time, not after the flesh of family knowledge but by the Spirit Who descended and remained upon Him like a dove. He continued his journey through the desert, through the wars, out of Egypt, beyond Sinai — all the way back to the beginning:

"Finally all backward motion ceased. He found himself standing before an obviously ancient gate. His heart was pounding, and his body trembled as he stood there considering his next move. He found himself reaching out to the heavy, weathered gate and giving it a tentative push. To his amazement, it swung open wide. Now he knew where he was. He had been drawn back to where it all began. He strode boldly through the gateway and found himself standing in the middle of the ancient garden. There a Presence was filling the place. It pulsated with an other-worldly reality. John knew that it was here that Adam walked and talked face-to-face with God. As he looked around, he saw a tree standing in a clearing. Carved into its bark, to his amazement, he saw the words, "God loves Adam."[5] John clears his throat, the scribe puts quill to parchment, and the old apostle starts, "In the beginning was the Word..."

The prophet asked, "Can a nation be born in a day?"[6] The simple answer is Yes-if that day is a day of revival. America was birthed in revival. Seeds sown from the days of the separatist Pilgrims, who left England's hearth carrying embers of revival once burning brightly and in whose breast lay the spark of Reformation that the just shall live by faith, form the foundation of our nation. Before the First Great Awakening the dry bones of the prior century had shriveled under lukewarm religion and dead tradition. But the seed was in the ground and at the scent of water the root put forth its shoots and budded. God poured out His Spirit. The colonial soil of Columbus and the Pilgrims was waking up to the destiny ordained by Him who carves out a nation's boundaries. Once again, like in the days of the Pilgrims religious dissent and dissenters became fashionable during the great awakenings in Western civilization. Devout men and patriots, their principles inspired by the vibration of the sound from heaven founded a nation under God. God was doing a new and living thing. At the set time, seeds laid down in primal revival appeared in full bloom. We see in America an example of the impact on human history primal revival can make.

Emphasis on Scripture and God's moral laws of governance were perceived to be rational elements upon which to build an earthly government. They were woven together to fashion the garments of law needed to clothe the nakedness of vanity and the frailty of human nature. Devout men, breathing the clean air of return to God, were all the more convinced on assurances received in revival meetings. Benjamin Franklin walked backwards through the crowds from Whitefield's preaching stand in order to calculate the number in attendance in a meeting. He counted 30,000. It was a small meeting that day. Patrick Henry, Sam Adams, James Madison, Washington, and many others had ears opened to the sound of the rain when it came. The first decisions to support a revolution, which was necessary for freedom of spirit and worship of God among equals, were drawn up in church halls. Among the social changes wrought in revival was a great emphasis on public education. Christians, realizing the need to eradicate ignorance and to instill values in their society, founded America's first public schools. It is a travesty that our learning institutions have become bastions of secularists and their ilk, denying God and seeking to twist future generations of Americans in their most formative and influential years. By the time our youth have run the dark gauntlet of 'higher education,' they have been subjugated to years of these false philosophies urging and inspiring them to turn their backs on God. It's time for a real revival.

The Awakening brought new understanding of our salvation covenant. It reversed the emphasis of the Puritans from "what God has done for man," to turn it around and enflame them with "what man can do in response to God." This affected their understanding of salvation and how to receive it. Suddenly man had power over his destiny, enabling him to lay hold of God Himself and become like Him if man so willed. This influence fed the democratization of Christianity in early America with a greater emphasis on the individual than had been made before. In those days that emphasis was on the responsibility and ability of the individual to impact the community, not the independent urge towards self expression common in post-modernity. Partly out of evangelical opposition to the deism associated with the French Revolution, the Second Great Awakening led by preachers like Charles Finney swept the northern United States. "Above all, revival is not a miracle in the sense of a physical change brought on solely by God, but a change of mind which, through influences of the Holy Spirit is ultimately a matter of the individual's free will," Finney declared. Armed with Calvinist influences suggesting all men are "moral free agents" who could obtain salvation through their own efforts of faith toward God at any moment, Finney persuaded many to believe, as he did, that time was running out for men to decide about their eternity. He ushered hundreds of thousands into the kingdom.

Perhaps prophetically Finney foresaw an approaching apocalypse of a more immediate sort. In the afternoon hours of Finney's ministry, civil war boiled over in America. Famous generals like Andrew Jackson experienced profound religious and moral personal metamorphosis under the preaching of Finney and others. The 'burned-over district' of New York State was the cradle of modern Pentecostalism. Women as well as men led crowded nightly prayer meetings. At "the anxious bench" sinners and backsliders confessed their sins. The preachers used plain language, including humor from the pulpit, in an effort to reach the common man with the uncommon message of the gospel. The fire of Pentecost was in full force, shaping and reshaping a nation one heart at a time.

The first Great Awakening revitalized religious piety and swept the American landscape between the 1730's and the 1770's. The

Second built upon it. Caught between those waves of awakening a generation came to grips with the rule of the King of heaven and threw off an earthly tyrant king. The United States is a modern example of the fruit of primal Pentecostal revival. Though its flame of revival has cooled for a moment the unction of its nativity has positioned America as leader among nations. That blessing is the birthright of those who seek the Lord and find Him.

Like Ezra and Nehemiah, preaching was only one rudiment of the fundamental reform revival wrought through men like George Whitefield. Social justice was the burning coal the fire of heaven laid on the hearth of the revivalist's hearts. Whitefield was among the first to preach to African Americans in his day. Black, white and brown found common ground, brotherhood and honor for one another at the foot of the cross. He was proactive among both orphans and suppressed minorities, awakening society to the plight of Native Americans and slaves. In many denominational circles slavery was denounced as sinful, and the First General Conference of Methodism concluded owning and keeping slaves was grounds for immediate expulsion. The Second Great Awakening was known as the "shopkeeper's millennium." The influence of the church meetinghouse affected churchgoers' work ethic and social habits in their daily lives. A culture was transformed. The rise of equality for women, respect for "the Sabbath" at the end of six work days, temperance, abolition, public education, and many other social reforms were spawned by that revival.

Once, community leaders, common folk, patriots, and pastors sought direction from heaven. Amidst spiritual stirrings men, oft upon their knees in prayer for direction, help, and blessing, set down present traditions of U.S. House and Senate opening prayers. This theme was revived a century later under the preaching of Finney when his 'new measures' upset old standards and broke open the way for abolition and equal rights for women. The heritage of both those great movements, spawned by God Himself, has been abducted by God haters and postmodern secularists. It's time for primal revival. Finney redrew lines of such religious fundamentals as covenant and how one receives salvation. They were revitalized with lasting effect in American theology and made an imprint on the face of our culture. The same way Luther spawned Protestantism with a living word, "the just shall live by faith," at a time when God Himself was breathing out those very words in heaven, Finney simply let his mouth be used to give God voice as he spoke. Church history changed national history forever.

The humanist religion of secularism has risen like a tyrant threatening to silence those who keep the command of God and have the testimony of Jesus. Faith, especially the faith of the Bible, is being banned from government and the public square in the West. Another kind of tyranny of faith is being imposed in the East. Nations languish under renegade leaders who deny God, the source of all authority, and reject human dignity. They are false custodians, surrogate parents if you will, of nations whom God formed and birthed. Those custodians may refuse to acknowledge the truth of their paternity for fear the features of Him who made them may begin to be seen upon the face of their public. But "God who made the world and everything in it is the Lord of heaven and earth and does not live in temples built by hands. And He is not served by human hands, as if He needed anything, because He Himself gives all men life and breath and everything else. From one man He made every nation of men, that they should inhabit the whole earth; and He determined the times set for them and the exact places where they should live. God did this so that men would seek Him and perhaps reach out for Him and find Him, though He is not far from each one of us. 'For in him we live and move and have our being.'"[7] And so we see that the purpose of God for every citizen of every nation is that men may seek God, reach out and find Him from the land of their birth! Pentecostal revival will bring a nation to its true birth: a nation under God of persons finding Him. "God, send laborers into the harvest'" is our prayer. Blessed are they who come in the name of the Lord. It's time for primal revival again.

Like the prodigal son, a person or a nation may have grasped the fortune of their inheritance and wasted it upon riotous living. We see this played out in present day America as well as in most of Western society. It is time to return home. It is time to seek the Lord. Nearly face down in the pig's trough, our sides ache with emptiness. The pods have left our eternal stomach hungry. Rife with division, darkness, disease, destruction, sin and confusion, we have come to the end of ourselves. We are ready to return home. Whole nations and suffering people groups are calling on heaven to save them. The land is ripe for revival. In the West, from record-breaking box office receipts for *The Passion of the Christ* to fisticuffs over a President's faith, America has God on its mind. A reporter for the Chicago Sun Times said popular culture is responding to the question posed on the cover of TIME magazine 40 years ago: Is God Dead? "Taking our clues from today's popular culture, the answer to the question appears to be a resounding 'No!' Standing around the water cooler or in line at Starbucks these days…" Falsani says conversations are as likely to discuss early Christianity and Biblical language as they are a popular television series or celebrity. She quotes a professor for religious research: "Any time there are these revival periods . . . the old meaning systems don't make sense for the majority of the people. There are so many changes going on in society that the traditional answers don't work. In any of those periods of tremendous and societal change, you're going to see a lot of this vitality. And in some sense, a disconnect from old organized authority. I really do think we're in an in-between stage or some sort of transitional phase where the religious reality that will be is not what it was."[8] This rift in our cultural fabric presents both opportunity and uncertainty. The opportunity for the hunger to be filled—the uncertainty of what the emptiness will be filled with. Hopefully, not with pig pods.

Revival is the way home for every soul. Revival restores us to our native land, that heavenly plane from whence we have fallen, the place of desire and communion, of ecstasy and fulfillment, the place of reunion with God, and reconciliation with one another. We need primal Pentecostal revival to produce primal revival results. Historically beginning with the first one in Acts, Pentecostal revival has brought about a general sense of compassion and human kindness in the cultures of those revived by it. Harmony, fellowship and energized ardor for one another produces justice and social reform, care for the infirm and elderly, and a return to lawful order. The Great Awakening during the 18th century and the Second Great Awakening in the 19th century were times of mass spiritual revival spawning new interest in the Christian faith in America and England. New denominations grew out of experiencing the first things as God had done them before. Large-scale social activism as well as pure and fresh modes of religious expression abounded. George Whitfield and the Wesley brothers John and Charles ushered in the Great Awakening as primal revival hit them as college students. The revival fire was carried to the West and brought nearly seventy-five percent of Americans together in a common understanding and practice of the Christian faith and life! We hear in these voices the sounds as in the streets of Jerusalem:

"When the people heard this, they were cut to the heart and said to Peter and the other apostles, "Brothers, what shall we do?" Peter replied, "Repent and be baptized, every one of you, in the name of Jesus Christ for the forgiveness of your sins. And you will receive the gift of the Holy Spirit. The promise is for you and your children and for all who are far off—for all whom the Lord our God will call." With many other words he warned them; and he pleaded with them, "Save yourselves from this corrupt generation." Those who accepted his message were baptized, and about three thousand were added to their number that day. They devoted themselves to the apostles' teaching and to the fellowship, to the breaking of bread and to prayer. Everyone was filled with awe, and many wonders and miraculous signs were done by the apostles. All the believers were together and had everything in common. Selling their possessions and goods, they gave to anyone as he had need. Every day they continued to meet together in the temple courts. They broke bread in their homes and ate together with glad and sincere hearts, praising God and enjoying the favor of all the people. And the Lord added to their number daily those who were being saved."9

The primal nature of those first moments in the Upper Room signifies the true nature of revival ongoing: by the power of the Spirit-not able to be produced or reproduced, sustained or retained by human flesh. One does not get an apple from the seed of an orange. The rushing wind, the tongues of fire, the ecstatic drunken effect of His presence, the inclusion of all nations, the spectacle, the stigma and the fruit of many lives transformed are the enduring features of Pentecostal revival. Prominent among those original features are ardent love for one another, swift departure from sin, conversion of sinners, social justice affecting the culture, and the spread of the Christian faith. Primal revival cannot be replicated in artifice or man-made constructs and be expected to produce life from death or salvation from sin in the manner that first Pentecost has done. Far from cultism or heresy, true revival is typified by something "new" to existing tradition, be it in emphasis or practice. It's not spawned in some newly rationalized set of ordinances. Revival is a coal of burning fire bursting from off heaven's altars, coming right out of the furnace of the living presence of God Himself, as seen by Daniel, John and Isaiah. It lands in the heart of the messenger and leaps to flame in his mouth. The former rains of revival marked dramatic social, economic and political reform from ancient Israel to the present day. But this revival will not be a passing one. It shall burn brighter and brighter as it ushers in His coming.

The believer's KEY to primal revival is the FIRE OF PENTECOST: If you want the fruit you must have the root. To experience its force you must drink from the source! The first revival was Pentecostal in signs and wonders and unusual miracles. "And suddenly there came a sound from heaven, as of a mighty rushing wind, and it filled the whole house where they were sitting." Acts 2:2

---

1 Genesis 1:2 *Five Books of Moses,* Everett Fox

2 Harvey Cox, *Fire From Heaven: The Rise of Pentecostal Spirituality and the Reshaping of Religion in the Twenty-first Century,* Reading: Addison-Wesley Publishing Company, 1994

3 Harvey Cox, *Fire From Heaven*

4 Don Milam, *The Ancient Language of Eden,* Shippensburg, PA, Destiny Image, 2003, 39

5 Ibid. 96

6 Isaiah 66:8

7 Acts of the Apostles 17:24-28

8 Catherine Falsani, Chicago Sun Times

9 Acts of the Apostles 2:37-47

CHAPTER TEN

Revival is Permanent

That day in the car, the Preacher asked a seventh time, "What is it about revival?" I had already heard more in those few moments than could be learned in a year, "What is it about revival?" I replied. The atmosphere around me changed. It seemed this answer would be more important than all the rest put together. "It's permanent," He told me. Suddenly the Man in the car was gone. Everything within and without went silent. All sound and distraction ceased. Even the air seemed to have been drawn away with His Presence. I was instantly sobered, my mind hushed like the weaned child David speaks of in the Psalms. I turned down the road to our house and pulled into the drive. A great weighty quiet ushered me out of my car and into our kitchen. Putting my things down on the table, I stood seeing nothing before me but His last answer. In a moment I heard myself say, "Lord, if revival is permanent why has one never lasted?"

In the 1980's we were part of the pastoral leadership of a church that received a visitation. The persons who welcomed and received that revival were changed forever. They still carry seeds of the God-life planted in them. Those seeds are fruit and healing for a new generation today. When that revival came many of the mid-wives of it were laymen not officially 'ordained' as part of the church leadership. Yet, they were anointed stewards of the new life being born in our midst. The church was like a woman pregnant with child. The body was birthing something that was a living manifestation of Someone. This was the first thing we learned in that visitation: revival is not a thing. Revival is the arrival of a Person. Our spiritual mentor Derek Prince had been in Spirit-filled ministry and missions for over forty years. He stated that that revival was the greatest visitation he had ever witnessed first hand. For many weeks hundreds of people arose in pre-dawn darkness day after day to gather corporately and wait in the Presence of God. Persons, including some on the pastoral staff, were convicted of hidden sins. Open confession and repentance was the norm. The fear of the Lord moved in to push out lukewarm religion and fill cold hearts. Deliverance, salvation and miracles abounded. Little children, grandparents and everyone between came to the sanctuary to get under the spout. Joy refreshed hearts and healed hurts. It overflowed into our daily lives. This was that prophesied by Joel, a true Pentecost in the 20th century.

Our order of service was disrupted. The priorities of our lives, natural and spiritual were rearranged by His Presence! Business as usual took on new measures and new protocols. There was more life and God-encounter in that sanctuary than in years of previous meetings combined. This was personal. This was experiential. This was supernatural and it was corporate. Unusual spiritual revelation included corporate open visions of the Cross planted in the sanctuary, the Blood flowing down for all to see. Young and old had meaningful and helpful dreams. Little children and laymen prophesied. Angels appeared bodily to many. It was messy. It was spontaneous. It cost us our pride, our convenience, and our schedules. It was glorious and joyous. Souls were saved and families restored. Women, who in our church tradition were restricted, prophesied freely. The faithfulness of years of service was rewarded overnight. Revival showed up like visiting family members often do: unannounced! It happened that we were in a time of a major pre-arranged transition in church leadership. Looking back now we understand that the revival gave opportunity to shape the transition in the grace and new life the visitation brought. Instead the revival and our 'business as usual' were uncomfortably juxtaposed. Some in the transitioning leadership were put off by an ongoing emphasis on repentance. The ordered chaos of the meetings encouraged laymen to take a lead. This posed some lack of clarity. It didn't necessarily set the tone in which to introduce the arriving persons into offices of leadership. Like wanting the new owner of a house to view the property with its best face forward there arose an urge to 'move on.' In short, we began to dig manmade channels in which the River should flow and expected the Holy Spirit would adjust His course.

While those in appointed office should always give direction to the flock, it is a much more delicate matter when giving direction to a sovereign visitation. For revival to remain, the stewards who host and nurture it must recognize the central Figure of revival is a Person. The Holy Spirit is under the impression He is God! Senior leadership bears a great responsibility when revival comes. Hosting revival is different from hosting church. It is an art not a science. You cannot manage it with a daytimer. An assumption that the Lion of Judah or the Rushing Spirit of God can be domesticated because He comes into our house was a misstep. We didn't realize that right away. The meetings went on. Our business proceeded. Then something else happened. If one listened closely, that otherworldly sound of revival became a clanging cymbal. As time passed interest divided, commitment waned, enthusiasm cooled. As the church returned to its old charismatic agenda, the midwives and laymen anointed for revival wept. We felt as if we'd lost a child. The new life born in our midst was gone. A grief lodged in our soul. Our lives were forever changed. We had tasted something no man could feed us. We would ever long to partake of that heavenly food again. It satisfied like nothing else but we knew not where to buy it. Revival was bittersweet, a memory. This is what we learned: revival is like God. Alive. No one gave Him His life and only He can lay it down. Revival is not a period of enthusiasm that makes a church or ministry grow. It is not an event where the music is louder, the preaching more passionate, the meetings longer and the gifts of the Spirit more evident. Like the child of parents, revival is living. Revival is born of One whose features and DNA it carries. We can have His life and Presence and be enfolded in all He is without reservation and without end when we recognize His knocking and say "Blessed is He who comes!" But once we open the door, like the elephant in the room, He sits where He wants and is rather hard to ignore!

Revival is the manifestation of God. Relationship with Him produces seeds of life in us. Relationship with God is the first calling of every son and daughter of God. Everything else flows out of that ongoing, vital love. The anointing for permanent revival comes from right relationship. Revival is as permanent and as Present as God Himself. He is holy. He is joy. He is salvation and power. He is creative. He is fruitful. He is peace. He is love. He bears, hopes, and believes all things! Revival has His eternal unchanging same yesterday-today-forever nature! We have to but recognize when He comes to us. We have only to step into His realm. Where He is recognized, welcomed, and given His throne, He settles down and revival becomes permanent. Adam was created for permanent, personal, intimate, relationship with God. People in right relationship are key to the abiding Presence of revival. People become the stewards of visitation. This is not an exclusive group. Anyone can be a part of the revival company God anoints to carry the seeds of visitation. But do not mistake hyper-activity or flakiness for revival just because it's different from the norm. God intended Adam to live forever in His Presence, eating the food of life He provided, enjoying permanent fellowship with Him. He also created Adam for a particular part in that process. Adam was to cultivate the seed God gave. The man and woman were meant to live forever in unbroken, face to face visitation every day. They were meant to eat from the harvest of life they tilled but something disrupted the relationship. Adam and Eve chose other food. The fellowship they had been created for with God and with one another was broken. Face to face visitation ended. Death entered. The man and his wife were sent away from the Life-giving Presence. But Adam did not lose his appointment as a tiller of God's seed. God had sown seed in the earth. The man He had made was created to bring forth that seed. So it is with revival and its stewards. The redemptive work of Christ is activated in us by the Holy Spirit. He makes ongoing vital relationship with God possible. The failure of the first Adam did not destroy the destiny of God's man. The Last Adam fully recovered both the man and his destiny. The sons of God are still His tillers in the earth. Do you know Him? Are you called by His Name? You carry His seeds of revival for this generation and the next. It all begins in your relationship with Him. You carry the wax-coated seeds of revival for this generation and the next.

A decade after God sowed the oil-rubbed seeds of revival into the desert of our religious landscape, soft sweet rains of refreshing began to fall from heaven. As those showers soaked into our lives, the revival seeds planted in us before began to germinate. Those shoots began to unfold in the soil of our lives. We learned that true revival carries seeds of life no man can give and no man can take away. We can ask for the rain in the time of rain. When the rain comes, revival seeds, even if it's been a hundred years since they were sown, will blossom again. Revival will flourish for a new generation. We are gardeners of the life God sows in the earth. We have inherited the God-life that Jesus carried and passed on to us in inheritance at Pentecost. In the hearts and under the hand of the stewards of revival those seeds can flourish in every season. Farmers will tell you that farmland can develop something called hardpan. Fertilizer, planting, trampling of the soil, and the depth of the tiller blades all have their effect. The cumulative impact season after season hardens the underlying earth. Left undisturbed those hidden layers can develop into an impenetrable layer of barren clay. Hardpan. It will eventually strip a field of fertility. New crops will fail. It is the same with our hearts. When we become callous or religious, insistent on doing things in a particular way according to certain tools and rules, or allow offenses to come, hardpan develops. Spiritual hardpan renders even prime topsoil barren. The roots of the plant cannot reach the nourishment they need. We yield less and less. We prevent others from bearing fruit. For revival to come it's time to break up our fallow ground. "If you will return, O Israel, return to Me," declares the LORD. "If you put your detestable idols out of my sight and no longer go astray, and if in a truthful, just and righteous way you swear, 'As surely as the LORD lives,' then the nations will be blessed by him and in him they will glory." This is what the LORD says to the men of Judah and to Jerusalem: "Break up your fallow ground and do not sow among thorns. Circumcise yourselves to the LORD, circumcise your hearts, you men of Judah and people of Jerusalem."[1]

The heart condition of God's people prepares us for His coming. The blessing of nations is contingent upon the condition of our hearts. Revival is relational. Repentance is the secret of right relationship. Repentance is a perpetual state of mind producing a change of heart. Revival necessitates and facilitates change beginning in God's people as He transforms them from glory to glory and builds them from strength to strength. If our response to His Presence and work become business as usual the spark of visitation will cool. Jesus showed us how to keep our hearts and steward the seeds of revival. Beginning with permanent, intimate relationship with God, the Last Adam farmed the seeds that ushered in revival. He received the seeds of prophetic fulfillment declared in Scripture. He broke up the ground of His own heart. He labored over the seeds of visitation in prayer until the life in those seeds burst forth in signs and wonders everywhere He went. He kept Himself in right relationship and the anointing flowed through Him without measure. "'The first man Adam became a living being.' The last Adam became a life-giving spirit. However, the spiritual is not first, but the natural, and afterward the spiritual. The first man was of the earth, made of dust; the second Man is the Lord from heaven. As was the man of dust, so also are those who are made of dust; and as is the heavenly Man, so also are those who are heavenly. And as we have borne the image of the man of dust, we shall also bear the image of the heavenly Man."[2] Jesus walked in daily, permanent repentance toward God and in right relationship with man. His right living and right thinking is what the Bible calls 'righteousness.'

Repentance prepares us for right relationship; right relationship with God and one another precipitates permanent revival. The fruit of a changed mind is a sanctified life. Sin quenches the free presence and power of the Lord. God abhors sin. But there is a vast difference between holiness and religion. Repentance and holiness are intrinsically related. The sanctifying work of the Holy Spirit continues as we live in repentance. Those who continue to walk in repentance continue to experience the renewing of their minds. Paul speaks of this in Romans 12 verse1: "I beseech you therefore, brethren, by the mercies of God, that you present your bodies (that means our mortal body, mind, and spirit) a living sacrifice, holy, acceptable to God, which is your reasonable service." He follows with further explanation of how one keeps himself from hardpan. "And do not be conformed to this world, but be transformed by the renewing of your mind, that you may prove what is that good and acceptable will of God." These are practical instructions for revival. The Godhead exists in permanent bonds of fellowship and mutual love, contributing one to another. This is the pattern for all creation. The anointing flows out of the community of the Godhead. It causes the many who receive the anointing to grow together into one. They become the habitation of visitation. Personal and corporate repentance produces love. It sets the stage for permanent revival in our lives. As God makes His habitation among His people, permanent relationship is forged. That dwelling place becomes the sanctuary for the thick glory of the Presence of the Lord. He comes to reside permanently! The sanctuary becomes an ark for revival. Those who do not recognize the sanctity of the ark will flit from place to place. Rather than strengthening the habitation of revival they muddy the waters of God's river for everyone. Repentance builds the sanctuary for revival. The foundation is permanent right relationship. When believers seek God in truth, recognizing, welcoming and responding to the His work, revival will flourish permanently.

A Farmer in His field, God is always working to bring up blossoming fruitful visitation. Unfortunately those laboring with Him are few! Revival people are the key. They are co-laborers with God and one another to nurture the seeds of revival. The stewards of revival determine its permanence. God is looking to separate His sanctuary from everything that can be shaken that He might dwell in our midst permanently. The world, the flesh, and the devil must go. The Lord spoke through Haggai and said that as the end of the age draws near, He will shake heaven and earth. The result is His temple is filled with shekinah as in the days of old. The Godhead gives us a clear example of what God intends in those who are called by His name. The Three Persons in One never change their address or Their relationship with one another! While legitimate circumstance in jobs or specific family needs and crisis are reasons to relocate from one city to another we must carefully consider the oft used saying, "The Holy Spirit led me to go here or there or led me to do such and such." We must see that the fruit of our guidance is consistent with the nature of the One leading us. Frequently changing churches, attending but never committing in one church family, never becoming a viable, loving, faithful contributor to the ongoing well being of a church family is inconsistent with the nature of God, our Father. Augustine recorded a hymn written by Victorius which exalted the Holy Spirit as the *patris et filii copula* "the bond of the Father and the Son." Augustine regarded the Spirit as "the bond of unity between Father and Son on the one hand, and between God and believers on the other. The Spirit is a gift, given by God, which unites believers both to God and to other believers. The Holy Spirit forges bonds of unity between believers, upon which the unity of the church ultimately depends. The church is the 'temple of the Holy Spirit' within which the Holy Spirit dwells. The same Spirit which binds together Father and Son in the unity of the Godhead also binds together believers in the unity of the church."[3]

A critical part of the foundation of permanent revival is being rooted not only in Jesus Christ by faith, but in a very practical way, being planted in a spiritual family. Our lives must be established on a surer foundation than individual 'experiences' alone. Relationship was one of the primary influences in early evangelism and church growth. Love and commitment is an outstanding feature of Pentecostal revival in the early centuries of Christianity. Biblical revival is not solely God's action or man's reaction. It is initiated by God and responded to by man. Both harmonize and synchronize as the Holy Spirit pours out grace. The choice is ours whether to step into the realm of His glory, or to just continue on our own path. God never changes. He remains ever present, ever caring, life giving, and all-powerful on an immediate day-to-day basis. His nature of love, joy and peace is constant and accessible. Since revival is a simple response to encounter with Him, we must realize that revival is always present, available and permanent!

The voice of Christ as John heard Him on the Isle of Patmos is "the sound of many waters." This is the sound of the multitudes in heaven and the voice of the living creatures. When they speak, deep calls unto deep. People hungry and thirsty for God come to the waters to drink from the life flowing out of them. Jesus said: "Anyone who is thirsty let him come to Me and drink and out of his belly will flow rivers of living water. This He spoke of the Holy Spirit." The church that was born on Pentecost is our first example of a church in revival. People were transformed in living encounters. The gospel exploded in that local revival and many were "added to the church daily." In the contemporary conference culture we have lost the blueprint of Scripture for the design of God's house. We are the living stones. We cannot claim to love God if we do not love the people around us. Love is relationship, ongoing, committed and faithful. A Christian must be connected to spiritual authority and fellow believers in a local church if he is to actively be connected to the Body. Without the counsel that comes from others including those we are accountable to, the guidance of our own spirit will fail. God sets the solitary in families. His house is a family home. Laying down our lives in service of one another builds God's house. A Christian living on their own, pursuing individual destiny can never be fully conformed to the image of Christ. Jesus laid His life down for the Church, one body made of many members —only the rebellious dwell in a dry land!!!

Like everything else in God, relationship, love, pure and simple, but not especially easy, is the secret of permanent revival. Revival contains a *contingency upon the ongoing heart condition of God's people.* "If My people who are called by My name will humble themselves and pray; seek My face and turn from their wicked ways then I will hear from heaven, will forgive their sins and turn and heal their land," is the famous revival cry of 2 Chronicles 7:14.

Jesus' habit was to go aside and spend the night in prayer to God. He kept watch over Himself and His generation. In the secret place He heard the parable of a sower who went out to sow. The seeds of heaven He received from consistent communion with the Father were life and visitation for future generations. They germinated in His life and heart. In whispered tones of conversation with the Father in the night watches, God made Him understand His part was to receive the seeds, watch over them faithfully, keep them pure and sow them into men's hearts. He sowed them into those around Him by relationship beginning with His family and disciples and sowing beyond into the generation that heard Him. Some fell on stony ground, some were devoured by birds, some were choked out by the cares of the world, but some fell on the good ground of 120 in relationship with Him. The rest was God's part as the rain of the Spirit came in showers of refreshing grace and confirming signs. The result was the power of Pentecost released for the next 2,000 years!

Revival is the ongoing effulgence of God breaking in upon our natural realm.[4] He intends the visitation we call revival to be perpetually occurring and re-occurring, a wheel moving and extending His kingdom. The prophets describe the glory of God moving over the earth on these wheels.[5] Revival refreshes, restores and raises up reapers for the harvest! "For there is hope for a tree, if it is cut down, that it will sprout again, and that its tender shoots will not cease. Though its root may grow old in the earth, and its stump may die in the ground, yet at the scent of water it will bud and bring forth branches like a plant."[6] It's time for the light of revival to shine forth in the darkness of this hour. The seed is in the ground. God has come to us like the rain. John saw the Spirit descend and remain upon Jesus. As we cultivate our hearts to live in permanent, right relationship with God and man, the Dove of God who rested in tongues of fire on the 120 will descend and remain on us.

The believer's KEY to living in permanent revival is RIGHT RELATIONSHIP: The anointing flows out of love for God demonstrated by our love for one another. Faithful, committed, interdependence with every joint supplying provides an ark for revival. "Beloved, let us love one another, for love is of God and everyone who loves is born of God." 1 John 4:6-8

---

[1] Jeremiah 4:3-4

[2] 1 Corinthians 15:45-49

[3] Christian Theology An Introduction, Alister McGrath pg. 313

[4] Effulgence: A brilliant radiance; resplendent; to shine out. This is one of Mahesh's favorite descriptions of the shekinah.

[5] See Isaiah, Ezekiel and Daniel's accounts of the throne in Scripture.

[6] Job 14:4-9

CHAPTER ELEVEN

Revival People

"In the year that King Uzziah died, I saw the Lord sitting on a throne, high and lifted up, and the train of His robe filled the temple. Above it stood seraphim; each one had six wings: with two he covered his face, and with two he flew. And one cried to another and said: 'Holy, holy, holy is the Lord of hosts; the whole earth is full of His glory!' And the posts of the door were shaken by the voice of him who cried out, and the house was filled with smoke. So I said: 'Woe is me, for I am undone! Because I am a man of unclean lips, and I dwell in the midst of a people of unclean lips; for my eyes have seen the King, the Lord of hosts." Then one of the seraphim flew to me, having in his hand a live coal which he had taken with tongs from the altar. And he touched my mouth with it and said:

'Behold, this has touched your lips; your iniquity is taken away, and your sin purged.' Also I heard the voice of the Lord saying: 'Whom shall I send, and who will go for Us' Then I said, 'Here am I! Send me.'"[1]

"The king is dead!" The morning news shocked the nation. Heralds ran from house to house, people stood in the streets, their hands hanging at their sides in disbelief. In the shops, in the government offices, in the house of worship, people held their heads and wondered what to do. The eleventh king of Judah had reigned

115

for half a century, more than any king before him. He subdued the nation's enemies, expanded its borders, and established its prosperity. Religion was on the rise. Then suddenly the greatest king since David was dead! An official in the administration, Isaiah was also nephew and friend. The tragic news that day shook the foundations of all those living in the land. As everything that could be shaken was being shaken, Isaiah saw the Lord. He had gone to the house of prayer to find solace and found instead, the King of kings was alive and well! The sound of mourners' dirges all around him was drowned out by the noisy shouts of worship coming from the throne. Men's faces all around him were full of shadows and confusion, but the faces of the ones beholding the Lord of glory shone like lightening. The strong ones of the nation were weakened and bowed down…but God was lifted up and those who saw Him flew in strength! The Voice that shook the foundations of the house was also the One they worshipped there. This was His doing, a sign that only the foundations of His throne could be certain. The mouthpiece of God put his hand over his mouth. "I am undone!" It wasn't the circumstances of earth that undid the prophet. It was revelation of the Man of heaven that changed his tune! All hope in man's systems fled. His trust was moved to settle on the Lord upon His throne! One of the holy messengers took a coal of fire from the altar where blood atoned for sin. With fire and blood he flew and touched the prophet's mouth. Isaiah's past disappeared into the smoke and he was set upon the new plane of his calling. He saw the people of the land in need of intervention, in need of visitation, hopeless without this revelation of the true King. The Voice of Many Waters spoke: "Whom shall I send, who will go for us?" The lips the coal had touched then answered, "Here am I, send me!"

Isaiah was in revival. Revival people possess a peace that passes human understanding, even in the midst of mortal trials. They cease from anxious striving; contentment and security comes from Him who is their All in All. Once they see the Lord of Glory, hear the creatures singing, and receive the knowledge of His will, revival people can't be moved. They become a rock for others, a refuge from the heat, a house upon the rock. Floods may come, rains may beat against its walls, it will not fall! Peace and direction for a world in labor pangs, refreshing in the face of the worst the world can offer, will be found in those who know heaven's joyful sound. They will be a sanctuary. Once revival touches them, revival people become a semblance of those creatures at the throne.

Their faces flash like lightening...

"As I was among the captives by the River Chebar, the heavens were opened and I saw visions of God. Then I looked, and behold, a whirlwind was coming out of the north, a great cloud with raging fire engulfing itself; and brightness was all around it and radiating out of its midst like the color of amber, out of the midst of the fire. Also from within it came the likeness of the four living creatures. And this was their appearance; they had the likeness of a man...And each one went straight forward; they went wherever the Spirit wanted to go, and they did not turn when they went. As for the likeness of the living creatures, their appearance was like burning coals of fire, like the appearance of torches going back and forth among the living creatures. The fire was bright, and out of the fire went lightening."[2]

Revival fire is sparked by revival people. They are drawn into God's fiery Presence. Moses insisted, "If You do not go with us we will not go up from here."[3] God responds, "My Presence will go with you and I will give you rest." Like Moses, revival people's countenance shines like lightening. The flame that sparked Azusa dropped from heaven's altars into the heart of a poor black man. Papa Seymour's 'face shown like lightening' in the sense that the glory was so strong around him, he hid his face behind a wooden crate. From there Seymour delivered the messages that stirred the hearts of all who heard him. The embers of that Holy Ghost blaze was carried in the censers of revival people and set the world on fire. The sparks revival people receive, flashing from the throne, are carried in their bosom and fanned into a flame. The flames grow into a whirlwind of radiating glory. When revival fire touched Isaiah's mouth he heard the call of God: "Who will go for Us?" Isaiah answered, "Here am I. Send me."

Revival people are ambassadors of God's heavenly realm. In John's revelation he expressly says that the anointed ones carry "the testimony of Jesus." Revival people, "like the appearance of a rainbow in a cloud on a rainy day" are surrounded by an atmosphere of miracles. The shekinah rested in a pillar of fire on the ancient ark and embodied signs and wonders. Revival people are soaked in the shekinah. They exude His glory. The miracle Presence of God sends out radiant rays of power. When the living creatures step into those rays they pick up ecstatic vibrations of revival. On those vibrations they are transported, from glory to glory and from place to place. The evangelist Phillip picked up those vibrations and was transported to another town to preach. If we receive and steward revival we are only a step away from entering the realm where impossible becomes possible and the unthinkable becomes an every day occurrence! Revival people carry the manifest Presence and are the forerunners of imminent visitation from God. Like John the Baptist, they come before Him to prepare the way for revival in many people's lives. They draw down the fire of God. Their faces shine with light from the glow of glory. Similar to the living creatures dwelling in the glory their "appearance is like burning coals of fire...the fire was bright and out of the fire went lightening." When revival people walk into a room filled with people, there is something different, an evident inner spark of God in them. When they speak the sound in their voice cries, "Holy!"

God has promised, "I will shake heaven and earth and fill this temple with My glory!" Isaiah saw that glory. Ezekiel saw that glory. Daniel saw that glory. The disciples saw that glory. They were shaken and cried, "Holy!" Holiness becomes the superconductor of His glorious power. The realm of glory calls revival people in and opens their eyes to the heavenly plane. God comes to His habitation with His winnowing fork is in His hand. He separates chaff from wheat and shakes all that can be shaken. His fire burns up all that is not holy. Revival people welcome the fire of God and succumb to its effect. They do not shirk from its cleansing power. The smoke of cleansing is like incense. It draws sinners to the altar and calls the wandering sons to come home. Revival people carry the spark of repentance that brings those "times of refreshing" promised by the Lord. They live near the veil where the four living creatures cry: "Holy, holy, holy is the Lord of Hosts; the whole earth is full of His glory!"

Isaiah shut his mouth. Ezekiel fell down. Daniel bowed. The disciples trembled. The living creatures ran. Revival people yield themselves like the living creatures. The Presence of God animates them completely. He surrounds and captures them so that in Him 'they live and move and have their being.' The creatures ran "back and forth in appearance like a flash of lightening." The apostles went everywhere preaching the gospel with signs and wonders. When they returned Jesus told them, "I saw Satan fall from heaven like lightening." Signs and wonders come from the glory realm. Signs and wonders destroy the power of the devil. Revival people pick up signs and wonders and transmit them to others. Revival people carry the lightening power of God. When they preach and when they heal, they reveal the Son of Man who comes like lightening flashing from the ends of the earth.

Obedience to the Father...

Power comes with obedience to the Father. As a mature son Jesus exemplifies obedience and power. Pure devotion to the will of the Father earned Jesus entrustment of true riches in the power of the heavenly kingdom exercised on earth. Jesus positioned Himself to live by the Spirit on the plane where the four living creatures hovered continually in the Presence of the throne worshiping the One who sat there. Jesus perspective for living day to day took command from Him. He making Himself utterly dependent upon the Holy Spirit, Jesus submitted to the revealed will of the Father. When Jesus was baptized it was to 'fulfill all obedience.' In turn the Spirit came on Him in fullness. Jesus was "led (some translations say driven) by the Spirit into the wilderness" for testing. He armed Himself with fasting prayer, putting His body and its desires and deeds of the flesh under the authority of the written word. Not to be swayed by temptation from the devil, He relied upon His Friend the Holy Spirit who had urged Him to go into the desert place. Without a second thought Jesus followed the cloud. In night watches, avoiding wild beasts, suffering heat and cold, hunger and thirst, Jesus overcame. He "returned (from the wilderness) in the power of the Spirit." His public ministry began with signs and wonders that testified God was with Him. Miracles confirmed the word He preached. Jesus had authority over sickness and demons. He had power to call down angels for assistance. He had gifts of discernment, words of knowledge, and anointing for prophecy. Moving in the anointing was second nature. Obedience, revelation, and power are symbiotic in revival people. Under the unction and guidance of the Holy Spirit the fruit of their lips has been touched with the coal from the altar. Led by the Spirit, their lives, body and mind, will be superconductors vibrating and emanating with the glory from the Presence on the throne. The Bible calls them the 'mature sons of God.'[4] They are men and women who constantly put to death the deeds of the body with its sinful nature and lower appetites. They are men and women who see with spirit eyes, hear with spirit ears, and speak the Spirit words. They go where the Spirit goes and are not put off by anything occurring on the earthly plane.

The Greek word for *led* is a present participle connoting a continuous action. This leading is not restricted to objective knowledge. The subjective promptings one receives for major decisions and 'unusual' actions should be discussed with spiritual overseers and reliable counselors to guard against mistakes.[5] The leading of the Spirit will never contradict the nature of God revealed in Scripture. Knowledge given by the Holy Spirit is easily entreated and peaceable. It will never contradict the revealed, written word of God. Furthermore, the prompting of the Spirit will build not destroy relationships. Being led by the Spirit is central to the lifestyle of revival people. The Holy Spirit is the Lord of revival people. They live in constant obedience to Him. Their minds are molded by Him. They go where He goes and stay where He stays. Like the four living creatures: "wherever the Spirit wanted to go, and they did not turn when they went."[6] Whatever He is doing; whatever He is saying; wherever He is moving; every time He turns, the fullness of their being goes with Him. Like the living creatures, revival people live where vibrations of the glory keep them in full blown ecstasy. As the creatures exclaim and testify, declaring what they see, this messy, spontaneous, glorious, joyous, revival moves across the earth. In worship they rise up on revelations of Him and run back and forth to do His will. They are God's tuning forks. They are constantly picking up revival and transmitting it to creation. They are in revival. Heaven is in revival. We are in revival…are you?

"Now as I looked at the living creatures, behold, a wheel was on the earth beside each living creature with its four faces. The appearance of the wheels and their workings was like the color beryl, and all four had the same likeness. The appearance of their workings was, as it were, a wheel in the middle of a wheel. When they moved, they went toward any one of four directions; they did not turn aside when they went. As for their rims, they were so high they were awesome; and their rims were full of eyes, all around the four of them. When the living creatures went, the wheels went beside them; and when the living creatures were lifted up from the earth, the wheels were lifted up. Wherever the spirit wanted to go, they went, because there the spirit went…." Ezekiel 1:15-21

The foundations of God's throne are wheels. Like God, a wheel has no beginning and no end. Instead, He *is* the Beginning and the End. In season and out God comes to us like the rain. He expects us to bring forth fruit of revival in every season. The wheel rims are "high and full of eyes all around." Revelation from God for any situation is available for the asking. He holds all things together by the word of His power. Revival people have their feet firmly planted on a foundation that cannot be moved. With one foot touching earth as intercessor and one planted in heaven as priest they wield the powerful, two-edged sword of God's word until it comes to pass. For revival people earthly circumstance is subject to the word of God, spoken, written, and settled in heaven. Their conviction, strength, knowledge and authority comes from the Lamb who sits on the throne. He is Savior. He is Lord. There is no realm, present or future, temporary or eternal, that is not provided for or subject to their King!

In the year king Uzziah died Isaiah saw the throne. Not the one on earth, he saw the throne in heaven. The kingdom of earth was in turmoil but the kingdom of heaven was in perfect peace. Isaiah saw the Lord, high and lifted up. The insolubility of His kingdom rested firm even though on earth "the posts of the door were shaken." They were shaken by the Voice of Him who cried out and the house was filled with smoke.[7] The pillars of the temple were no small timbers. The whole edifice of massive stones was upheld by them. Revival people are the pillars of God's habitation.

Opposites dwell together...

God's throne is mobile. He traverses the earth at will. But He is also steadfast and immoveable. This is the mystery of God: opposites reside together in His glory. The living creatures depict the mystery of opposites dwelling together: "As for their likeness, each had the face of a man, a lion, an ox, and an eagle." A man and an eagle are natural opposites. One traverses heaven the other walks on earth. The four living creatures have both arms and wings; they walk and they fly. The lion and the ox are natural enemies. One is the predator and one is the prey. In the glory these opposing natures dwell together in harmony and power. This mystery is the hope of the nations. The glory of God is the one solution to problems the human condition wreaks among the sons of men. Revival brings the glory. Who can make natural enemies to be at peace with one another? Only God. Not history of Him or theory about Him, but a living, vital, immediate encounter with Him. One like Ezekiel had; like Daniel had; like Isaiah had; like John had. Ezekiel saw the Lord in glory while he was in exile as a prisoner of Israel's enemies. Daniel saw the Lord in glory while serving as a slave of a powerful pagan king. Isaiah saw the Lord in a time of turmoil and sudden death. John saw the Lord of glory while in chains on an Island. In the glorious living Presence the solution for all human conflict and every human problem is revealed. Opposites dwell together in God! He is the Lion and the Lamb. He is the Beginning and the End. And He is the same unchangeable, permanently faithful, righteous, joyous God! It is that God who visits the earth when Pentecostal revival comes in its season. Isaiah prophesied according to the visitation:

"There shall come forth a Rod from the stem of Jesse, and a Branch shall grow out of his roots. The Spirit of the Lord shall rest upon Him, the Spirit of wisdom and understanding, the Spirit of counsel and might, the Spirit of knowledge and of the fear of the Lord. His delight is in the fear of the Lord, and He shall not judge by the sight of His eyes, nor decide by the hearing of His ears; but with righteousness He shall judge the poor, and decide with equity for the meek of the earth; He shall strike the earth with the rod of His mouth and with the breath of His lips He shall slay the wicked. Righteousness shall be the belt of His loins, and faithfulness the belt of His waist. 'The wolf also shall dwell with the lamb, the leopard shall lie down with the young goat, the calf and the young lion and fatling together; and a little child shall lead them. The cow and the bear shall graze; their young ones shall lie down together; and the lion shall eat straw like the ox. The nursing child shall play by the cobra's hole, and the weaned child shall put his hand in the viper's den. They shall not hurt nor destroy in all My holy mountain, for the earth shall be full of the knowledge of the Lord as the waters cover the sea. And in that day there shall be a Root of Jesse, Who shall stand as a banner to the people; for the Gentiles shall seek Him, and His resting place shall be glorious.'"8

In the glory, by the Spirit, natural enemies lie down side by side in peace and every child on earth is safe from harm. This is revival. The Root of Jesse is the answer. Beginning at the Root, God has provided a peace process for Jerusalem, for Judea and Samaria, for the uttermost parts of the earth. Peace between God and man. Peace between man and man with whom God is reconciled. We see from Scripture that the righteousness world systems hunger for is only found in God. Social justice, compassion, peace and prosperity come from the glory. His habitation will be glorious. His habitation is revival!

Anointed with the glory...

It is time for us to see the Lord in His glory. It is time for revival in every life, every family, every city, every church and nation. A return to harmony with God through revival will bring a cloudburst of supernatural intervention. Accompanied by miracles and salvation, the healing effect of such an advent will turn nations and restore clarity. Let every man, woman, and child whose heart is bent on pilgrimage heed the call of Joel. It's time to seek the Lord. Ask for the rain. The visitation of revival and the manifestation of the glory of God on earth is the answer the world seeks now. That visitation begins with you, where you are today. This is the day of your visitation. This is your day of salvation. God is seeking revival people. If you hear His voice, do not harden your heart. Only believe and step into His Presence. From time to time revival people can slip through the veil into the misty cloud where He abides. Once they've tasted His glory nothing can keep them away. The distance between living in the vibration coming from earth, wracked with the struggle of lost men's souls, or being connected to the Presence in His glory is one tiny step. God is. Revival has come.

Revival people realize they are ministers of heaven's kingdom. They carry that environment and establish it around themselves in spite of the culture of the world where they are. The anointing of Christ as it flowed through His disciples set people free from the oppression of evil spirits. In the anointing, the disciples healed all kinds of diseases. They were moving in revival glory. Jesus said, "If I cast out demons by the finger of God, surely the kingdom of God has come upon you"[ix] Three essentials of every revival from Pentecost to Azusa are: a prevailing spirit of corporate prayer; Pentecostal infilling of the Holy Spirit; and perpetual soul winning. The first is the most essential aspect of receiving, maintaining and giving away revival. The last is the obvious fruit of that revival. And the second is the link between the two. The person, power and presence of the Holy Spirit is the essence of revival. He is the central Figure of revival glory. First to last, beginning to end, in the past, for the present and in the future, the Lord is the Spirit and the Spirit of the Lord is revival!

"A voice as clear as a bell answered, 'I don't go away. My people go away from Me...'"

It is a word to all who are connected to His presence, to all who are thirsty and to whoever wants to come. It is a word to those who tend the watch fires of His altar all around the globe. He is calling today, calling revival people to spread the ancient flame. We carry revival. Revival does not carry us. The Man on the throne asked the question, "Who will go for Us?" With fire in his mouth, Isaiah answered, "Here am I. Send Me!"

The KEY for revival people is FLEXIBILITY: The Welsh revival was sparked when a young man named Evan Roberts prayed, "Bend me, O Lord," and received the Holy Spirit. Revival brings change. Revival people bend with the wind. They are flexible and steadfast at the same time. The world is entering her final hour. Shaking is coming. The flexible people who carry revival are like the sons of Issachar: they know the times and seasons, and they know what to do!

---

1 Isaiah 6:1-9

2 Ezekiel 1:1,4-5,12-13

3 Exodus 33:15

4 Romans 8:14

5 See footnote NKJV *Spirit Filled Life Bible* Nelson, pg. 1700

6 Ezekiel 1:20

7 Isaiah 6:3-4

8 Isaiah 11:1-10

CHAPTER TWELVE

Watching for Revival

...then as if He placed a thoughtful hand upon His chin and pondered the rest of His answer, the Man said, "That's why I think maybe watchmen could sustain one."

Elijah was a watchman revivalist. We find him in 1 Kings 19 travailing like a woman in labor as he prays for revival rains to pour over his nation. Paralleling the spiritual climate in Israel at the time, God had closed the heavens, and no rain fell on Israel's soil for three years. God tells Elijah to inform the wicked king that it is time for rain. In an act reminiscent of the libation ceremony at Sukkot, Elijah pours twelve jars of water over the altar. Fire from heaven strikes and the hearts of the people turn as they fall on their faces and cry, "The Lord, He is God! The Lord, He is God!"[1] Elijah does not stop to bask in the first spark of revival, however. He watches for the rain.[2] "Come let us return to the Lord for He has torn us but He will heal us; He has stricken, but He will bind us up. After two days He will revive us. On the third day He will raise us up, that we may live in His sight. Let us know, let us pursue the knowledge of the Lord. His going forth is established as the morning; He will come to us like rain, like the latter and the former rain to the earth." Hosea 6:1-3

The prophet Hosea appeared at a time when anarchy, lurking beneath the topsoil of the kingdom of Israel, had begun to rear its ugly head. The nation had reached a zenith of power under

Jeroboam II, but was slipping into decline. Outward trappings of peace, prosperity and plenty were fading. Corrupt leadership, unstable family life, widespread immorality, class hatred and poverty all sown in seasons of turning from God were bearing their bitter fruit. Caught up in the pursuit of happiness, Israel had departed from her First Love, her Redeemer-God. The heart of the nation had strayed and her ears had grown dull to hearing from heaven. She no longer answered when He called. The people, and even the priests, still kept up rigorous religion, but their worship was a mixture of unbelief, idolatry, and tradition while justice, truth and mercy had flown. Political collapse was just a few short years away. As with an adulterous wife, Israel's infidelity was her chief sin. God's merciful solution to this dire situation is to exhibit His faithfulness to her by sending His revival. This is a pattern of God's deliverance when we are found in this position, whether as an individual or a nation. God does not cast Israel away forever, but visits her. Together with his contemporary Amos, Hosea calls for a return from many lovers to one God. He emphasizes the supremacy of God's moral law as Israel's foundation. In the case of Hosea, God's prophet became the sermon. God tells His messenger, "Go love a woman who is beloved of many lovers." Hosea finds the harlot Gomer and takes her for his wife. Gomer bears the prophet a son, a daughter, and a second son, all named prophetically for the fruit born out of Israel's backsliding. The very act of conception and the children that are born were living pictures of God sowing His love into Israel while she in turn brought forth fruit worthy of judgment. The message unfolds further when Gomer, even after bearing children to Hosea, abandons home and husband to run after other lovers. God sends Hosea to buy her back, and Gomer is subjected to a period deprived of intimacy. This wilderness experience brings her to the end of herself. The unfaithful wife realizes, in the same way the prodigal son comes to himself in the pig's trough, her first love was the true love. Hosea speaks prophetically to the nation, "The children of Israel shall abide many days without king or sacrifice…afterward they shall return and seek the Lord their God and David their king." Revival comes to her like the rain.

During this time we see the beautiful way in which God deals with the object of His affection. Hosea is the tragic love story with a happy ending. "I will allure her and bring her into the wilderness and speak to her heart. I will give her her vineyards from there. And the Valley of Trouble shall become a door of hope." This is the quintessential context in which revival visits the earth. Hosea prophesies that the merciful rain shall cause the seeds of right-eousness that God Himself has sown in the earth to sprout. He declares that the nation's heart shall be betrothed to the Lord and the permanent union will cause abundance and rejoicing of a plen-teous harvest. "Come let us return to the Lord for He has torn but He will heal us. After two days he will revive us and on the third day He will raise us up that we may live in His sight. He will come to us like the rain-the former and the latter rain to the earth." This is the nature of God revealed. The rain is a picture of the outpour-ing of the Spirit to turn dry bones into living flesh. Revival is the proof of God's unfailing love. As the rains of revival begin to fall, the nation awakes from its dark sleep. Revival turns the hearts of His people back to Him and ushers in the fullness of His kingdom. Like the living message of Hosea, God has chosen us to dwell in the intimacy of revival. The Man in the car had said, "I don't go away….My people go away from Me….that is why I think *maybe* watchmen could sustain one." We think about the watchmen that have co-labored with us for many years. Keeping the watch as a church family every week from watch headquarters, they have learned the permanent practice of His presence. Stepping into the glory of corporate prayer and worship, they are transformed. Like Ezekiel by the River Chebar, watchmen connect to an eternal real-ity that supersedes their present natural actuality. Their eyes and hearts serve as conduits through which heaven touches earth. This is revival.

When God brought His children out of Egypt, when Habakkuk sat on the ramparts waiting for the Word of the Lord, when Jesus laid down His life in prayer, when God prepares to do something new among His people, we are instructed to watch. Watching draws us through the veil and engages us in the river of His purpose coming from the throne. When God instructed Gideon to go out against the Midianites, He only chose men who watched as they drank. This is a message to the Church. As we contend for culture-changing revival and living water of revival bubbles up in our midst, God is seeking watchmen. Watchmen are people fully engaged in the purpose of God on a daily basis. They do not simply stop at the river for a drink, but watch for the command to act. Those three hundred men that Gideon took to battle were not necessarily the most charismatic leaders, nor the most aggressive on the battlefield. They carried instinctive discipline to watch. We have seen this phenomena usher in world-changing transformation in the past. In 1857, a businessman in New York named Jeremiah Lamphier wrote in his journal, "…as I was walking along the streets, the idea was suggested to my mind that an hour of prayer, from twelve to one o'clock would be beneficial to businessmen."[3] In obedience to this leading, Lamphier started a prayer meeting at the North Dutch Reformed Church on Fulton Street in Manhattan. The hour-long meeting was unpretentious and flavored with the efficiency of the business district in which it was birthed. However, this simple act of corporate prayer soon exploded. Soon the entire district was filled with noon-time prayer. Thousands experienced miracles of healing and salvation. An estimated one million people turned to Christ in this revival.

In 1989, a protracted prayer meeting of watchmen transformed the political and social climate of Europe. Faithful watchmen had been holding weekly prayer meetings in Communist Leipzig, East Germany for a decade. Suddenly, they found themselves in the current of a mighty move of God. Who moved? Was it Him alone? Or was it their prayers? The two, heaven and earth harmonizing brought revival down. After the prayer meetings, people would light candles and walk peacefully through the city streets, a gentle protest against the Communist regime. Political change was in the air, and these meetings began to grow. As many as 50,000 eventually joined in! Then came October 9, what Germans call "the turning point." The East German government got involved, sending in police and soldiers with orders to shoot the protesters. Many feared a bloodbath. When one church opened its doors for the weekly prayer meeting, two thousand Communist Party members rushed in to take all the seats. No problem: the church opened the balconies for the regular gatherers and, like it or not, the Communists had to sit through a prayer meeting! Amazingly, shots weren't fired that night in Leipzig as 70,000 people marched peacefully through town. Or the next Monday, when 120,000 marched. Or the next, when there were 500,000—nearly the entire population of Leipzig. Many German Christians believe prayer silenced the weapons. In early November nearly a million marched through the nation's capital, East Berlin. Police defied orders to shoot. Churches on both sides of the wall harmonized together in prayer. Filing out into the streets to hold their candle-lit vigils, they prayed that the wall would fall down. The vibration began to crack the social and political foundations that built the wall. The president resigned in disgrace, and soon there was an opening in the famous Berlin Wall. The stunning development spread throughout Eastern Europe as peaceful revolutions dismantled Communist regimes.

What had these prayer meetings wrought? The New Republic reported, "Whether or not prayers really move mountains, they certainly mobilized the population of Leipzig." Sindermann, one of the leaders of the old GDR regime, said before his death: "We had planned everything. We were prepared for any eventuality. Any except for candles and prayers."[2] Certainly there were political and social undercurrents, but don't miss the spiritual dimension. It was obvious to the people most closely involved. The language of prayer silenced all other tongues. "Give ear to my prayer, O God, and do not hide Yourself from my supplication…Because of the voice of the enemy, because of the oppression of the wicked; destroy, O Lord, and divide their tongues, for I have seen violence and strife in the city."[3] A friend of ours lived in Berlin at the time of these events. He reported to us that on the night that the wall was breached there was a wedding on the eastern side. At the conclusion of the wedding, the bride and groom went out into the streets where they led a procession of their guests and bridal party in seeking the freedom of their nation. They were joined by more and more people. A swell of victory buoyed up the crowd as a rumor began to swirl through the candle-lit procession that the government had announced the end of travel restrictions on East-Berliners. The joyful crowd pressed themselves to the nearest checkpoint, where bewildered guards, not sure what to do and whether to believe the reports of the people, simply opened the gates! Our friend recounts that in the midst of the jubilation of the moment, he watched as an old Pentecostal watchman, in his youth a trumpeter in the military, was hoisted up on the wall with his trumpet where he displayed his praise to the One who had won with a hymn. A few weeks after that dramatic "turning point," someone put up a banner in Leipzig, "Wir danken Dir, Kirche," it read, "We thank you, church."[4]

Watchmen are always at the ready, waiting to respond to the next move of God. They tap into the realm of faith where nothing is impossible. Revival people are like this. They live in the glory. They possess the sense of having already laid hold of the fruit of victory. Hezekiah changed God's mind through prayer. Elijah changed the seasons through prayer. Jeremiah and Daniel changed history through prayer. Peter and Paul were released from prison through prayer. Jesus changed the destiny of mankind in prayer while on His face in the Garden. When He stood up He had gained the victory of the Cross. It was then just a matter of walking it out!

Our watchman's handbook *Set a Watch: Every House a House of Prayer* is the fruit of years of growth and development of a prayer watch. There is a distinct understanding of discipline developed in keeping the watch—permanently. It lays an apostolic foundation that will not change with season or circumstance. According to what the Man in the car said, it might just be a vehicle for the glory of God to touch nations. This is the foundation from which the history of Germany was changed. From this foundation Jesus spoke to Peter, 'the rock,' on the night He was betrayed. The Gospel of Matthew recounts this moving scene in chapter 26. The regular cadence of the four men's footsteps was accompanied by heavy breathing as they neared the top of the steep path. Silvery light sliced across the rocky terrain, broken by shadows of the gnarled olive branches for which this place was named. Each man was silent, yet the poignant question passed down by Moses' command, "Why is this night different from all the other nights?" reverberated in their heads. Wrapping His cloak closer to His side, the Rabbi paused, sorrowful eyes met the souls of His closest companions. He asked them to watch and pray. Their gaze followed Him as He continued on to His accustomed place of prayer. The three men sensed His urgent call, but eyes heavy and bellies full from the Seder meal, they quietly succumbed to the lethargy of sleep and their muttered prayers slipped into fervent snores.

In His hour of deepest sorrow, Jesus turns to His friends and says, "My soul is exceedingly sorrowful, even to death. Stay here and watch with Me."[5] Generations before, the Lord instructed His children to keep vigil, watching through the night, for on that night He had promised to visit His people with a mighty deliverance. The Lamb to which that Passover night was pointing asks no different of His most intimate companions when He invites them to watch with Him in the Garden of prayer. When Jesus finds them sleeping, He asks, "What? Could you not watch with Me one hour?"[6] The spirit is willing, but the flesh indeed is weak. Jesus relied on the watch to overcome the weakness of His flesh, subjecting it to the authority of His willing spirit under the hand of God. How much more should we? Jesus' intent on that night in the garden had not been solitude. We read of several other accounts where Jesus went off by himself to pray, but this night, He desired the help of His friends. As with the nature of God who is mysteriously Three Persons together in the bond of love as One, the primordial aspect of revival is community. While one can live in permanent personal revival, an individual alone cannot sustain visitation for a generation. A harmonious community watching and praying together will. The day of the lone ranger Christian so characteristic of the revival waves of the 60's, 80's, and 90's, is over. God is taking away the masks and shooting those wild horses! The body of Christ is one made of many interconnected, interdependent, permanent members. The human body reflects the body of Christ. It is not an ethereal symbolism. Real flesh and blood, functioning corporately together, make up the body. The centrality of the local church has been negated, neglected, used, and abused, by previous contemporary movements. In the last days, both God and His glory filled with signs and wonders will dwell where He has always intended — within the embrace of the one He died for, His bride. God's address is "house of prayer for all people." His home is the local church. The essential nature of community is described in Don Milam's *Ancient Language*: "The ancient language of Eden required a communal setting for its development. Without a community the mother tongue would disappear. Language cannot exist apart from the culture formed by community. In the midst of community people shared the feelings of their hearts and the creative ideas formed in their thoughts. This mutual sharing of thoughts and feelings, thoughts and ideas, enhanced the vocabulary of the ancient language and empowered by the community. Any attempt to restrict and repress the mutuality of this life would destroy the original language of Eden."[7] This is the essential secret of why the watch is more vital, supernatural, practical, fresh, and enduring. Community is the reason the watch is spreading. One man alone, or even a thousand independent individuals, will not effectively steward the seeds of visitation for a generation. A body of members, even a small one, can receive, germinate, and birth that seed, ensuring there will be a second generation of blessing coming after.

Likewise, watchmen are people fully engaged in the purpose of God on a daily basis. They have learned, like Brother Lawrence, to practice the Presence in all that they do.[8] Like Bonnie in her car as she drove home, like John on the Isle of Patmos, like Hosea's door of hope, revival glory is eternally accessible. Scripture tells us that the glory of the knowledge of the Lord will fill the earth.[9] Watchmen are positioned to usher revival in to every atmosphere in which they find themselves. Rather than retreating to an isolated island utopia called "revival," watchmen are integrated into the fabric of the society where they are found. They are true watchmen in the sense that they have their eyes and ears stationed in the gates and on the ramparts of their culture. This is part of the framework and permanence that is needed for a sustained revival. Duncan Campbell said, "An evangelistic campaign or special meeting is not revival. In a successful evangelistic campaign there will be hundreds or even thousands of people making decisions for Jesus Christ, but the community remains untouched... In revival, God moves in the district. Suddenly, the community becomes God conscious."[10] May we take this statement further? In permanent revival, communities will be filled with revival people: watchmen who continue to function as gate-keepers and visionaries in secular society. Permanence is attained when the Church does not abandon her role in society, but sets her sight on shaping the culture for generations to come. What does it take for revival to break out where you are? The instigation of revival is not very complicated. In Scotland two elderly women refused to let go the hem of God's garment for their nation. This resulted in the historic Hebrides revival. In Jerusalem, 120 people watched and waited *until*. The result: Pentecost continuing to this day. The Lord told Solomon "If My People who are called by My Name will humble themselves and pray and seek My face and turn from their wicked ways THEN I will hear…I will forgive…I will heal."[11] As Solomon prayed Glory filled the Temple.[12] Revival is the healing of every person, every family, every church, every city, every nation, every people group on earth. Our part in that healing begins with the biggest word in human potential: *if*. "If My people." God did not say *when*; God said *if*. That indicates that there is an aspect of the advent of revival that rests with us. The greatest American revivalist Charles Finney said something profound about the true nature of a genuine revival: "Revival is not a miracle in the sense of a physical change brought on solely by God, but a change of mind which, through influences of the Holy Spirit, is ultimately a matter of the individual's free will." Think about that. Our free will, your free will determines revival. Following that *if* are four simple steps within the reach of every person, pastor, laymen, or national leader: humbling, praying, seeking, turning. In the spring of 1986 led the National Day of Prayer in Washington, DC. In a visitation from heaven he saw end-time revival in the manner of Azusa coming on the nations. The recipients of this revival would be, *"humble, holy and hungry."*[13] Christians, not pagans, Christians, not the devil or demons, Christians, the people called by His Name, hold the power of revival and visitation. There are three evidences in the life of a man in revival. Do you want revival? This is what you must do:

Justice

"He has shown you O man what is good and what the Lord doth require of thee: Do justice, love kindness and walk humbly with thy God."[14] It is amazing how complicated we make the simple and powerful truths of God. The tripod of justice, kindness and faith prophesied by Micah is necessary in revival that changes nations.

One without the other two, two without the third will not do it. To effect heaven on earth all three together, social justice worked through kindness, inspired and empowered by ongoing relationship with God are needed and are civilization's only hope. Every religion in the world seeks to construct difficult systems by which a man may sanctify himself and draw near to God. Whether they realize it or not, they are in search of the power of His presence in their life. But God says it's easy. Social justice is essential for righteousness, beginning with right dealings in our immediate personal sphere such as family and employees or employers. Social justice alone can become a religion, but it can never bring revival. In fact, true revival ultimately produces social justice not the other way around. The great freedoms and rights enjoyed by women and African Americans in the U.S. are a direct result of the Finney revivals. The Second Great Awakening was known as "shopkeeper's millennium" because of the influence of the church meetinghouse on churchgoers' work ethic and social habits in the marketplaces. The rise of equality for women, respect for "the Sabbath" at the end of six work days, temperance, abolition, public education, and many other social reforms were spawned by that revival. True revival produces something. Biblical revival causes the turning of a nation and brings about restoration in a society. It has long lasting effects. In the 21st century we are in desperate need of a genuine revival of Biblical proportions.

Kindness

Just as a social gospel will not initiate revival, neither will simple compassion and good works towards others. A whole society committed to 'random acts of kindness' will not bring revival to a nation. It may change the general social climate from oppressive to pleasant, but it will not usher in a visitation that confronts the soul, reveals the Savior, and causes personal acknowledgment of Him. In his lectures on revival during the Second Great Awakening,

Finney observed that the need for revival is indicated by a "want of brotherly love and Christian confidence" among those who profess 'religion'. When the zeal and fire to share the faith with unbelievers wanes it is time for revival. When Christians have lost their love for one another it is time for revival. There is a kindness that precipitates revival. Social change, beginning with self, is the simple but powerful fruit of the kindness of God flourishing in the hearts of those who received His visitation. Cultural transformation has been wrought by revival from the time of the first century church through the Second Great Awakening. In ancient Rome, revival people cared for the dying and nursed the sick during the great plagues of olden times. They had no fear of sickness or death for they knew the Redeemer and were certain of a better and lasting reward. The revived ones seek to show kindness to the poor, to liberate the oppressed, to heal the broken hearted, to declare their day of visitation from on high. Christians who had been revived sought justice for enslaved classes. They no longer saw the color of skin and sought equality for man made in God's image. They worked to eradicate ignorance and injustice through eradicating the disadvantage that ignorance played in keeping classes separate and bound to prejudice and fear. Who can deny it is time for revival in education East to West? *Madrassas* in the East promulgate hatred, racial and gender prejudice; public universities in the West indoctrinate the youth to spurn God and throw off all forms of obedience to His righteousness. America's first public schools were founded by Christians revived in visitation of Pentecost. It is a travesty that American institutions of 'higher education,' many of which were founded in response to revival, have become bastions of godless philosophy. These very branches of seeds sown in the First and Second Great Awakenings are now denying God and promoting moral anarchy among our youth during their most formative and influential time of development. Revival brings heaven to earth and anoints those who carry it to live a life free from bondage to the laws of human nature. It's time for a real revival.

Humility

What are the signs of revival? Sometimes the indicators of revival are the very worst possible seasons and circumstances in human experience. When we have come to the utter end of ourselves and are unable to lift our heads He comes. He is the glory and the lifter of our heads.[15] For David, He was the Lord of the dance. When the Great Host of the wedding supper to surpass all wedding suppers steps in to give rest to His beloved, revival is here. Jesus' first appeared in a stable. He "made himself of no reputation...and after being found in the appearance of a man, He humbled Himself and became obedient to the point of death, even death on a cross."[16] Permanent visitation will rest on the people who embrace the humility of Christ. The spirit of humility will be evident in our attitude toward our local church. Jesus did what He saw the Father doing, and He was the consummate servant. He washed His disciple's feet and "learned obedience by what He suffered."[17] Every saint who desires to be found in the middle of what God is doing or about to do in a generation should seek the place to be planted as a functioning, contributing joint in the body of Christ. Revival, like Christianity, is practical. People were transformed through encounter with the gospel that exploded in the revival of Acts 2. They were "added to the church daily." Contemporary Christianity tends to redraw the design of God's Church. If He walked among us today, Jesus probably wouldn't recognize it. He sets the solitary in *families*! We have noticed once born into a family, always a member of that family. When difficulties arise and heartaches offend you have to deal with them. This in fact is Christ. This is love. This is humility.

Perhaps today is a good time to review the basics. Do you flit from place to place seeking exciting experience? Can members of

Christ's body count on you? Find your spiritual tribe. Fit into the family God brings you to. Put down your root. Make yourself a "joint that supplies" for the edification of the whole. This may mean inconvenience and sacrifice. Jesus submitted Himself to the Father in a very specific and daily manner. He made Himself interdependent upon the Holy Spirit though He had in Himself the ability to operate on His own as God! He made Himself an accessible servant of those around Him, and thus fulfilled His calling and pleased the Father. God has historic things in mind. Let us do all we can to avail ourselves of His fullest intention. While we pray for the rain in the time of rain, let us not neglect the foundations upon which a lasting habitation is built! Whether you have known the Lord and gone away or never called upon Him at all, perhaps you have followed and worshipped other gods besides the Living God, He is speaking to you today. You may be a believer who is weary and worn. Disappointments may have hardened your heart. Mistreatment or miscommunication may have persuaded you to withdraw from fellowship. It's time to return to the Lord. He is calling you back. He is calling you home. There is a tree in the ancient garden. It is carved in simple letters "Jesus loves Me." Written on the palms of Him Who hung on the tree of Calvary are the letters of your name. You can step through the ancient gate into His glorious Presence. He has come to revive your life.

Seven times Elijah prayed. He heard the sound of rain. "Then it came to pass the seventh time, that he said, 'there is a cloud, as small as a man's hand, rising out of the sea!'" The sky blackened, clouds and wind rolled in, and there came a heavy rain to end the years of draught. Elijah stood and faced the coming storm. Wrapping himself in his cloak, he girded his loins and ran! Seven times the Man asked the question in the car, "What is it about revival?" Messy, spontaneous, costly, glorious, joyous, rewarding, permanent revival is waiting. Open your mouth and call. At Azusa street Papa Seymour asked for tongues of fire. When heaven answered, glory came down and set the world ablaze. The earth is in her greatest hour. Her greatest hour of trial; her greatest hour of glory. These two opposing realities clash on revival's shore. Friends and enemies grapple in the garden of prayer. Jesus is waiting for us there. We see Him under the olives, His countenance dripping with passion, His body bent in prayer. He still seeks His friends to watch with Him and gain the victory there. Like Jeremiah we see the Almond tree blooming and hear the Lord of Revival say: "I Am watching, waking, hastening, anticipating, sleepless, alert, vigilant to perform My word!"[18] It will be a short time now-perhaps just one hour. "Rise, let us be going."

The believer's KEY to watching for revival can be found in our WATCH MANUAL: For more than a decade Mahesh and Bonnie have lived the watch together with their church family at watch headquarters in Charlotte, NC. We have put the powerful keys to watching for revival in Set A Watch: Every House A House Of Prayer. This anointed handbook of guidelines, testimonies, prophetic perspective, prayers, CDs, DVDs, and special 'toolkit' will equip you as a watchman for revival. Set a Watch is available at our online bookstore: www.maheshchavda.com.

Prayer for Revival

Blessed are those who hunger and thirst for righteousness, for they shall be filled. Matthew 5:6

Father, in the name of Jesus I come thirsting for You. I cry out for Your Holy Presence to sweep over me. I repent on behalf of myself, my family, my church and my nation. I put away sins and forsake all that hinders me from entering Your glorious presence. I am desperate for You. I surrender my heart to Your holiness and mercy. Lord, hear my cry, I pray. Pour out Your Spirit upon me. Anoint me in Your glory and fill my hungry heart. I pray Your glory would come in and fill my heart, my home, my church. Make us Your house of prayer. I pray for signs, wonders and miracles confirming the resurrected Christ. I ask for living revival to be permanent in my life. I commit myself now afresh to You. May I serve the Lamb and proclaim His glory to the nations. Welcome precious Holy Spirit. I am Your dwelling place. In Jesus name, Amen.

[1] 1 Kings 19:39-44

[2] Eva Bell, "When Candles Broke the Wall" *Deccan Herald* (Nov 9, 2003), http://www.deccanherald.com/deccanherald/nov09/at1.asp

[3] Psalm 55:1,3,9

[4] Peterson, *100 Amazing Answers to Prayer*

[5] Matthew 26:38

[6] Matthew 26:40-41

[7] Don Milam, *The Ancient Language of Eden*, Destiny Image, Shippensburg, PA, 2003, 57.

[8] Brother Lawrence, a 17th Century monk, lived a life of practicing his presence in the midst of his daily activity which is described in his book, *The Practice of the Presence of God.*

[9] Habakkuk 2:14

[10] Duncan Campbell, "When the Mountains Flowed Down", Transcription of message to students at Faith Mission Bible College in Edinburgh, Scotland. http://www.revival-library.org/index.html?http://www.revival-library.org/catalogues/twentieth/campbelld/title.htm

[11] 2 Chronicles 7:14

[12] 2 Chronicles 7:1

[13] Mahesh and Bonnie Chavda, *Watch of the Lord*, Charisma House 1999, 2.

[14] Micah 6:8

[15] Psalm 3:3

[16] Philippians 2:7-8

[17] Hebrew 5:8

Watching for Revival!

Wheel Within A Wheel

Words and Music by Ruth Heflin

There's a wheel within a wheel, and it's turning in me. It's turn..ing in me. Its turn.....ing in me. There's a wheel...... within a wheel, and it's turn....ing in me. It's turning in the glo.............................ry.................................. .

2. There's a fire within a fire,
   And it's burning in me.
   It's burning in me.
   It's burning in me.
   There's a fire within the fire
   And it's burning in me.
   It's burning in the glory.

3. I can see. I can see.
   I can see the glory.
   I can see the glory.
   I can see the glory.
   I can see. I can see.
   I can see the glory.
   I can see the glory.

4. You are. You are.
   You are my glory.
   You are my glory.
   You are my glory.
   You are. You are.
   You are my glory.
   You are my glory.

This song was written by Ruth Ward Heflin a great revivalist of the last century who lived in permanent revival and sowed the seeds of it in others for more than half a century. She has seen the glory of the Lord!

Other Books available at our online bookstore: www.maheshchavda.com

Set a Watch: Every House a House of Prayer

Set a Watch: Every House a House of Prayer is your spiritual handbook to equip and anoint you to live in permanent revival. The fruit of more than a decade of committed, consistent, corporate watching and praying at The Watch of the Lord™ headquarters here in Charlotte, NC, this living selection of prophetic teaching and instruction will transform your home into a house of prayer! With over 15 hours of anointed teaching and worship CDs and over 200 pages of articles, prayers, testimonies and practical instruction, *Set a Watch* is a comprehensive equipper's manual to help you fulfill Jesus' mandate to Watch and Pray!

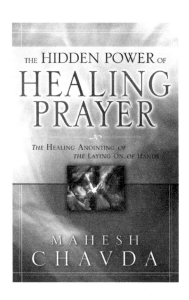

The Hidden Power of Healing Prayer

Here is the fatal blow to the belief that God does not heal today. Through the power of his personal experience and the strength of his Biblical insight, Mahesh Chavda reveals how the healing compassion of our Lord reaches the hurting masses simply by the believer's healing touch. Written with compassion, humor and insight, this book affirms that the healing anointing and the gifts of signs and wonders are not reserved for "super saints" or the specially gifted, but are available to every believer who carries the compassion and love of the Lord Jesus.

The Hidden Power of Prayer and Fasting

God has provided a way to turn certain defeat into awesome victory and demonic strongholds into highways of His love and power. When overwhelming defeat looks you in the face, whether the attack is physical, family, or financial crisis, The Hidden Power of Prayer and Fasting holds keys that will unlock the resident power of the Holy Spirit within you! International Best Seller!

The Hidden Power of Speaking in Tongues

"I thank God I Speak in tongues more than you all." Spoken by the apostle Paul in 1 Corinthians 14:18. In Mahesh Chavda's new book The Hidden Power of Speaking in Tongues, we are once again reminded and carefully taught about the incredible possibilities available in speaking in tongues. This spiritual gift, much maligned and controversial in our day, was a vibrant and necessary part of the worship and intercession of the early Church. It is an experience that hungry believers long to rediscover here in the twenty-first-century Church, as millions search for a more meaningful understanding and relationship with their Lord.

As he softly removes the mystique and mystery overshadowing this glorious gift, Chavda challenges the Body of Christ to pursue afresh the secret dynamic of speaking in tongues.

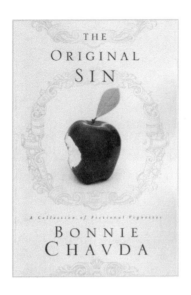

The Original Sin

The Original Sin is a collection of fictional vignettes full of intrigue, deception, power, hope, and love. Each compelling story chronicles the journey of the original sin in the hearts of humanity. They reveal the disastrous results that can arise when jealousy injects its poison into the lifeblood of humankind; but they also offer the hope and redemption that comes when we respond to God.

You will be enchanted by these dramatic stories as you witness the deceptive pull of jealousy in the lives of Cain and Abel, Sarah and Hagar, and Judas. The Stories of these biblical characters are a warning, reminding us that the original sin is always knocking at the door of our hearts, and that we must overcome it.

You may visit our bookstore at www.maheshchavda.com, or call toll-free 1-800-730-6264 to order by phone. Ask to receive our detailed catalog offering products from our ministry.

To contact us or for information about our Ministry see our website www.maheshchavda.com or contact us:

Mahesh Chavda Ministries
PO Box 411008
Charlotte, NC 28241
Phone: (704) 543-7272
Fax: (704) 541-5300
E-mail: info@.maheshchavda.com